Overpowering Nemo

Encountering Deliverance and Walking in Freedom

Ginny Burgin

malcolm down
PUBLISHING

Endorsements

What an amazing book! A demonstration not only of God's kindness but also His power to set people free by His Spirit and by His Word. Ginny's book will inspire many and supply the hope that many long for.
Terry Virgo (founder of the Newfrontiers group of churches)

Ginny has a remarkable prophetic gifting. *Overpowering Nemo* describes Ginny's story of how God's truth and power transformed her past tragic, suicidal life, to a new one of becoming a significant prophetic voice among the Newfrontiers family of churches. A must-read for all those who want to experience God's transforming power themselves.
Steve Brading (church planter and prophetic leader working among the Newfrontiers group of churches)

An important part of the ministry of Jesus was 'to set at liberty those who [were] oppressed' (Luke 4:18, NKJV). Ginny Burgin's book *Overpowering Nemo* is an excellent demonstration of the fact that Jesus' ministry in this respect continues today through His Church in the power of the Holy Spirit. Her story is an urgent reminder to the Church to reach out and not neglect the ministry of healing and deliverance for those who have been so abused and ill-treated. I commend this important book to you.
David Devenish (team leader, Newfrontiers Together)

Overpowering Nemo is Ginny's story of growing up in a set of very abusive relationships, and the self-destructive hopelessness and bondage this produced in her own life. Yet, it is the story of how Jesus came to her in that dark place and in His redeeming love led her on a remarkable journey of salvation, deliverance and healing.

I strongly recommend her book to anyone who desires to grow in relationship with the One who sets the captives free.
Samuel Poe (part of the leadership team at New Frontiers Church, Portsmouth, NH, USA)

We have known Ginny for many years and been privileged to team with her in ministry. There is a unique peace and beauty about her which, on knowing her story, is all the more remarkable. Her love for Jesus is clear and she possesses such a heart for others to find and experience freedom and healing.

This captivating book reminds us that what is impossible for man is always possible for God. It brings into sharp focus the full effects of the grace and power of God, turning the ashes of our past into a crown of beauty and causing our hearts to worship our glorious Jesus, the 'Man in the Picture'.
Rob and Helen Coleman (Grace Church, Bolton)

This is a very timely and much-needed testimony of God's transforming power and the practical outworking of walking free from physical, emotional, mental and spiritual abuse. It is personal and heart-aching and yet will resonate with anyone who has been bound by lies and hurts from the past or the present. It encourages us to step into the future with freedom, knowing we have a voice that is heard by a Father who loves us.
Graham and Fiona Tipping (City Church Sheffield)

After God intervened in Ginny's life, leading her to faith and to meet her husband, Stuart, they both came along to join the church we were leading at that time. This book details the powerful account of Ginny's experience in finding deliverance and freedom from a difficult and painful upbringing. After seeing her so powerfully set free from the grip of the enemy, we watched as God began to develop her life and

ministry, and saw her prophetic ministry grow. In those days of the coming of the charismatic renewal she brought some very important prophetic words to us, which helped to develop us into the strong charismatic church we later became. Today Stuart and Ginny have been married for many years and Ginny now teaches and ministers for many churches in the UK and abroad as part of her prophetic calling. This book is comprehensive and powerful and is well worth reading.
Ray and Jean Booth (retired church leaders)

This is a powerful account of one woman's journey from darkness into light. Ginny's backstory of abuse, of being 'shut down' as a person, leads into a truly inspirational story of deliverance and freedom – an eye-opening revelation of what God can do in a person's life. Honest, uplifting, unforgettable, a must-read for those who are looking for hope that God sets the captives free today.
Sheila Jacobs (editor and award-winning author)

First published 2020 by Malcolm Down Publishing Ltd
www.malcolmdown.co.uk

24 23 22 21 20 7 6 5 4 3 2 1

British Library Cataloguing in Publication Data
A catalogue record for this book is available from the British Library.

ISBN 978-1-912863-66-2

Cover design by Esther Kotecha
Art direction by Sarah Grace

Printed in the UK

Acknowledgements

A huge thank you to Anna Goodman, an author in her own right, who has sat with me, listened to me, cried with me, prayed with me, cajoled me, encouraged me, and helped me to get my story onto paper. Without Anna, this book may never have got to print. Thank you, Anna.

Contents

Preface

I have written this book using some of my own story, but not just because I want to tell the story for its own sake; it isn't meant to just be 'a testimony'. Rather, I wanted to set out how God can break into all of our stories in a way which sets us free, that the power of His Spirit at work in our lives is ultimately what we all need. I have interjected the story with those things that He has taught me over the years and I sincerely hope that what has become the whole book will help you in your own story of walking in freedom.

Ginny

Foreword

The world's most expensive vase is the eighteenth-century Qianlong porcelain vase. It sold for $53m. It is both beautiful and fragile. The world's tallest building is the Burj Khalifa, it's 828m high. It can be found in Dubai.

Now imagine taking the Qionlong vase and dropping it off the top of Burj Khalifa. Do you think it would be repairable?

When I began to spend time with Ginny listening to her story, I was left without words. She was that vase. Physically, emotionally, spiritually and psychologically she had been dropped from great heights and left to shatter into a thousand pieces.

Yet here she was, telling me her life story from a position of healing and forgiveness. There was no bitterness, anger or resentment, as one might expect. There was only a heart to help others experience the same restoration that she had so clearly received.

As someone with a background in neuroscience, I was fascinated. I know how fragile the human brain is. I know how formative those early years are. One might think she had reached a point of no return, a place of irreversible damage. But as Ginny so passionately articulates, there are no hopeless cases when it comes to God. He can do anything, with Him the impossible is possible. And it is true – Ginny is living proof.

The story you are about to read is deeply moving. It is a story of contrasts – darkness and light, lies and truth, captivity and freedom and finally sorrow and joy. Ultimately, it is a story about a God who exchanges evil for good.

Throughout this book, in amongst her experiences, Ginny weaves the lessons that she has learned - the truths that she has walked in, daily, that enable her to experience this 'great exchange'.

I pray that as you read the following pages, the Holy Spirit would do something deep in your heart so that you would receive everything that He wants to share with you and teach you through the life of this incredible woman. This is a story for you and this is a story for the Church.

May you be blessed in every way as you read it.

> A bruised reed he will not break, and a smouldering wick he will not snuff out, till he has brought justice through to victory. In his name the nations will put their hope.
> (Matthew 12:20)

Anna Goodman (Author of Connected: God's quiet voice in a world that shouts*)*

Introduction

God shapes and forms things out of nothing. He takes nothing to make something which brings glory to His name. 'Isn't it obvious that God deliberately chose men and women that the culture overlooks and exploits and abuses, chose these "nobodies" to expose the hollow pretensions of the "somebodies"?' (1 Corinthians 1:28, *MSG*).

Many of us come to Him as 'nobodies', nothing, with no identity – *Nemo* (Latin for 'no man' or 'nobody') – and many of us struggle to overcome in areas like depression, negative thinking and the difficulty in seeing ourselves as having a voice in any positive way.

But God is about calling, shaping, and forming a body which will ultimately become His glorious bride, His Church, bringing glory to His name. We are not meant to remain 'nobodies', overpowered by and still 'walking in the empty way of life inherited from our forefathers' (1 Peter 1:18, my paraphrase) but by His grace we are to overpower that which is of the 'old self' (Romans 6:6) and rise up to become part of that glorious Church and to give us a voice to speak to this chaotic world.

This is my reason for writing this book, to provoke you to trust God for His supernatural intervention in your life, to overpower whatever is your *Nemo* and to enable you to become a voice that will be heard. I have no need in myself to write any of this down, it is not some kind of 'cathartic exercise', rather it is about provoking you to have an expectancy for God to break into your life and make it new. It has been a battle to write this book, a battle to overcome that instinct to stay invisible, to let no one glimpse any of the shame, the trauma, the battles that once tried, and still sometimes do try, to keep me imprisoned in fear and silence.

But it is time now for speaking, for having a voice, for letting the world hear of the mighty power of God to bring about deliverance and freedom. It is a time to rise above the political correctness and intimidation which exists all around us in order to minister a supernatural gospel of grace to a hurting and fractured society. In short, it is a time for the Church to have a voice, to shake off invisibility and speak up as a prophetic voice to the world. It is a time for you to break free and find your voice. We worship a God who is able to move on our behalf, a God who breaks in as the Lord of Breakthrough, who can come with acts of supernatural power and miracles. This is the one who we worship, a God who sets the prisoners free (Psalm 146:7) and then uses those same prisoners, those who have encountered His grace and power, His comfort, to then minister that grace and comfort to others.

But it is not about trying to be 'somebody'. 'Nobodies' instinctively try to become 'somebodies', but that is not the answer.

To shift from the mindset of 'no one sees me, no one hears me, I am invisible' to 'everyone must see me, everyone must hear me, I am all important' is simply to shift from one aspect of pride and self-absorption to another. The answer lies in being freed from our self-absorption, to absorb ourselves in the One who shapes and forms and changes us 'from one degree of glory to another' (2 Corinthians 3:18, ESV) as we delight in walking out our every day with Him. So, the antidote to feeling like a nobody is not to seek to be a somebody, but to focus on Him who chooses nobodies to destroy what the somebodies consider important.

'Oh, but you don't understand, I've had such a difficult time,' you say, or 'But I'm still trying to come to terms with my father abandoning me' or 'I'll never be able to overcome that' or 'I'm comfortable with being a nobody', or any number of other reasons too numerous to list here.

But I do understand. I was a nobody. I was *Nemo*.

Chapter One:
The Presence of 'Nobody'

I once saw an advertising hoarding that read 'The Presence of the Absence' which I mused upon for a long time. In the absence of identity, approval, attachment, love and care, something else roots itself in one's inner being. This feeds on the loneliness, the shame, the guilt, the fears, and becomes a very real presence in itself. The presence of absence.

I suppose for me this presence began to name itself early on as I listened to my grandfather's ramblings.

I'm the eldest of three – there was me, a brother and a sister; six years between me and my youngest sibling. I was born into a lower working-class family in 1954, the year the food rationing stopped. Although the war had finished in 1945, it was still very difficult with a lot of hardship and poverty around until well into the 1960s. There were a lot of people around who had very little. Our family were just another poor family; we lived hand-to-mouth with very little food and the cast-off clothes of others in what amounted to slum conditions.

Mother did National Service in the Women's Land Army and Father did his National Service and then signed up for the regular army. So, my parents met, courted by letter and then they married in their early twenties having only known one another for a short time, mostly by letter, and having met just a few times.

Father perhaps didn't realise it at the time, but mother had severe learning difficulties. She had personality disorders too, the most notable being narcissism. She had absolutely no sense of responsibility for anybody around her, she just had a bias towards protecting herself; looking out for herself, her own needs, wants and desires. Father, on the other hand, was outwardly quite a shy man, seemingly a gentle soul to the outsider, yet underneath was a whirlpool of boiling rage. He'd had a very strict upbringing as my grandfather modelled his parenting on his own turbulent past. Father was very, very intelligent, a member of MENSA (a society for those who have a high IQ), though he was never allowed to do anything with that intelligence. In his family, you just went to work to earn a living, because that's what mattered back then – the fact that you had money in your hands to feed your family. So began the marriage of two very different people; mismatched both in personality and in intellect.

There you have the basis of what became real difficulty as one begins to see the concept of the 'sins of the fathers' (see Exodus 20:5) being worked out down through the generations.

Mother's parents lived in another town. I only really saw them a handful of times over my growing up years because people just didn't travel around as readily back then. My paternal grandfather had a two-bedroom bungalow that housed him, my grandma, Father and my young uncle. Later, my grandma's mother needed looking after as she'd developed dementia, and then Father brought his new wife to join them as well. Then I was born. So, in this small, two-bedroom bungalow you had my grandma, my grandfather, my grandma's ailing mother, my uncle, my mother and father and finally, me.

Seven of us living in a two-bedroom bungalow.

When I was coming up to three years old, my parents discovered that 'number two' child was on the way and so my grandfather bought a pair of semi-detached cottages. They were very basic; each house had two bedrooms, an outside toilet, no heating and no hot running water, just a cold tap in the kitchen. My grandfather, grandma's mother, grandma and uncle moved into one house and I lived next door with Mother and Father and eventually with my brother and sister. So that was the set-up.

I spent a lot of time with my grandfather and grandmother because they were the nearest things I had to 'normal' relatives. When it was just me, or me and my brother as a tiny baby, they used to take me out and about with them – those times were quite enjoyable. But from when I was very young I would listen to my grandfather talking about his growing-up years and his life story, and if you wanted one word for it, it was the word:

'*Nobody.*'

He was born in 1904 from a wealthy landowning family in Bedfordshire. In those days, if an unmarried woman had a child it was like *the* biggest sin, especially in wealthier families. The woman would be whisked away under the pretext of being at a finishing school, or having gone on a world tour or something, then she would give birth and return without the baby, all hidden away as a big secret. That's what happened to my great-grandmother. So, my grandfather's mother came up to Yorkshire, gave birth to him then left him with a family to bring him up and went back to Bedfordshire, and he never saw or heard from his birth family ever again, though he took on his mother's surname as his legal name.

He was brought up very strictly by his new family and then at a very early age he was given up to another family. It was in this second family where he began his schooling and grew up using their name, even though he was never legally adopted by them. So, he had a legal name that had to appear on official papers and he had another name that everybody knew him by. But he didn't belong anywhere; he had no idea who his birth mother was, nor who his birth father was, and the family bringing him up didn't really want him; they were just being paid to look after him. It was a sad story. My grandfather would often tell of his longing to have known who his mother was and would finish off his conversation with: 'I am a nobody; I don't even know who or what my real identity is.'

And the 'nobody' complex gradually set itself up in me.

The tragic thing is, many years later, well into my own adulthood, when my grandfather eventually died and was buried with my grandmother, nothing was ever altered on the headstone to say that he had been buried there as well. So that gravestone, even now, has no mention of him on it.

It was like he never existed.

Anyway, Grandfather used to talk about his strict upbringing and how his folks 'took the belt to him' and stuff like that. When I got a bit older, he would sometimes talk about his remorse about taking the belt to my father. I think he knew that Father was 'taking the belt' to me and that's why he and my grandmother tried to look out for me a bit. Maybe he felt a bit responsible for it going down the family line, I don't know. The Bible talks about 'the sins of the fathers being visited upon the children' (Exodus 34:6-7, my paraphrase) and sadly, we can often trace things back to previous generations, with the hurts and pains that they suffered recreating themselves in our own time.

Grandfather would sometimes talk about God as if he were exploring whether He might be 'out there somewhere', but it was all very negative; he took comfort in his nonentity almost as if he were proud of it, and I began to hide in it with him.

You may ask yourself, why should taking comfort from being like a nobody be 'pride'? Surely it's a standpoint of humility? And why would seeking to be better, to be 'somebody' also be pride? Surely it's good to counter the things that keep us cowed? Hiding in my nonentity is pride because I am looking inward to my own self, finding comfort there in my own self-sufficiency and my own misery. If I try to snap out of that, the tendency can be to try to achieve, to be 'somebody,' but that can just be another form of self-absorption. When I am self-absorbed like this I am less aware of God; I am not looking outward to the God of all history, a God of all time and space who holds everything in His hands, including me.

However, I never really thought about the existence of God in those days. It was simply a matter of surviving another day and I never had those types of chats with my grandma. She would just quietly make me something to eat when I turned up, knowing I wouldn't have eaten anything and was hungry; she knew that we weren't really being properly fed at home. Grandma would just cook me egg and chips and give me a drink. To this day, from time to time, I love to have egg and chips. She was a quiet, inoffensive lady who very much preferred to remain in the background.

These two people were the most 'normal relationships', I had and being alone with them was the nearest that I had to family normality. Unfortunately, my mother didn't like me being with them; she tried to prevent it and often it caused trouble for me.

One of the notable things about Mother was that she was a pathological liar. She lived in her own fantasies. But there was always a very, very, small grain of truth in the middle of the fantasy – it was usually built around something. For instance, she would say that she 'worked as a midwife', but she didn't; she worked as a cleaner in a maternity hospital. Or, she 'worked as a chef' in a particular pub, but actually she worked in the kitchen of a pub for a little while doing the washing up. I think she believed her own fantasies and lies.

Over the years I learned to see through the falseness of people around me, the way that people said one thing yet meant another, the way that people 'put on an act' when underneath that was not who they really were. I developed a yearning for there to be openness, honesty and genuine relating, for people to be who they said they were and therefore able to be trusted. But back then I only learned to mistrust everyone and everything they said.

Mother only ever had work for a matter of weeks because she wasn't capable of keeping a job. So, much of her life she didn't work, though it wasn't abnormal in those days for women not to work, but she wasn't at home looking after the three of us, either. If she did manage to work and earn money, she never saw it as something to help with the family finances; she just saw it as 'I'll have a good time with this' money. She'd buy herself a lovely frock, or some latest thing in clothing or jewellery. She adored jewellery, despite the fact that we, her children, didn't just get 'hand-me-downs'; we got 'hand-me-downs-from-the-hand-me-downs'!

Even these things set themselves up in the unconscious self – things like 'I don't deserve new things', 'I should only have what is left over', the new, the sparkling, the eye-catching, well, 'that's for someone other than me, I'm a nobody, it's not for me'. *Nemo* developed its presence more every day.

Father probably got frustrated as he couldn't have a normal conversation with Mother. He was a 'bottler-upper', keeping all his thoughts and feelings tightly bottled up, and I learned to do that well from him. I learned quickly that it was always better to keep quiet and *never* be heard.

When I was born, I think that in my mother's eyes, I somehow became a threat to her relationship with my father; I came between them in some way. She therefore had this funny idea that she had to get my father to not like me, or to 'lose it' with me, in order to keep her place in his eyes. I know that sounds weird. It's like him beating me somehow said to her that he cared about her more than he cared about me.

Mother was very devious, devising mind games or rituals to control and manipulate me to do or say what she wanted. Most of the time I saw her with a green 'aura' around her that frightened and silenced me. I didn't know then that I was being confronted by 'principalities [and] powers' (Ephesians 6:12, NKJV), things I didn't understand then, spiritual things, so I just lived with them threatening me. One thing I know now is that anything which manipulates, threatens and seeks to control is never anything other than the work of the enemy.

So, mother would do things and play mind games with me that would result in my father losing his temper and beating me. And when Father lost his temper, he just couldn't hold it in, he would be overtaken by burning rage and until he'd worn himself out, he just couldn't stop himself. He would hit me with whatever was near to hand; his belt, his boot, his book – and a lamp base on one occasion. He would lash out, kick, using whatever he could pick up first. It always went on and on until he was exhausted and I was in some semi-conscious state of pain and detachment. And then when he'd worn himself out beating me, he would retreat into solitude and my mother would have found some sort of pleasure in it all. I was the only one that he'd take his temper out on like that and it pleased Mother.

Mother never had any sense of responsibility in terms of how she should look after children, so she didn't feed us regularly or very well. She wasn't very good at doing the family meal at the end of the day when my father came home from work; sometimes she cooked – weird things, such as baked beans on Weetabix – sometimes she didn't. Often my father would come home and have to start making dinner for himself, and he wasn't the best cook either! He would get cross if there weren't any 'basics' in the house to make something from. He would also get cross if the house was a mess. And, of course, the house *would* be in a mess, it would be untidy; there would be dishes in the sink, wet washing all over the place and the laundry that hadn't been ironed would fill the cupboard until the doors would burst open. I quickly became the one who did the chores all the time, I suppose as a form of self-protection. I did them because my mother made me, but I also did them to do whatever I could to try to preserve peace and prevent Father from losing his temper. I lived with permanent anxiety, with permanent 'butterflies' in my stomach, with a readiness to try everything to avoid a beating or confrontation of any kind. I'd get so overwhelmed by the panic that breathing would become difficult and I'd just end up being sick and adding to the whole problem.

In the early days I'd always be thinking, 'If I do this or that, he might not lose his temper today and then I won't get beaten', yet eventually I didn't even think that way; I just behaved according to the pattern that had been set. At that time I didn't realise just how much Mother's mind games were affecting me.

I was born before my parents actually planned to have children, though unbeknown to me at the time I was their second pregnancy. They hadn't managed to get themselves financially established and back then you'd normally try to get a council property before starting a family. I think Mother resented the fact that I came along when I did, and then the sheer frustration of life meant Father didn't cope; that's when he lost it and beat me. I'm sure as a child I did things that were naughty, but I can't remember those times because I was always trying my best to behave well because I knew what would happen if I didn't.

Chapter Two: No Hopeless Cases

Later in life I was to discover that God is my Father but it took a long, long, time to realise that His love and His discipline did not mean anger, beatings and pain. For years my view of Father God was modelled on my earthly father. Somewhere deep down I constantly waited for God to trip me up, catch me out and mete out to me some painful circumstance to have to bear, that being His child meant constantly suffering pain, difficulty and anguish. Somehow the Bible's message of a loving heavenly Father escaped my notice. I was always trying my best to please Him because I knew I was bad and undeserving of anything good. I thought that if I put one foot out of line He would instantly be there to reprimand and 'beat' me in some kind of way. I believed that bad things would happen if I wasn't so very obedient to everything written in His Word.

How many of us live out our Christian lives like this? Overwhelmed by anxieties, never really finding our identity, our voice, just cowering under what we are used to and have always known. It can seem so much easier to believe the same old thoughts, the same old voices and behaviour patterns than to choose to turn around and begin to overpower them and embrace the new creation that God would form in us, and sometimes we can't do it anyway without the deliverance that comes from Him. I remember a character in a film, or on TV – I don't recall – saying that if you did not offload trauma it would come back to you like a demon, and to be sure demons can root themselves in us long before we come to Christ, hiding away, particularly under our Western culture, often disguising themselves as health issues or personality types.

But because of God's grace and mercy at work in us we can be freed and learn to unlearn the things we have been programmed to believe by our old life, overturning those things by leaning towards what is true and choosing to believe that. The Bible tells us of death and life and how we are no longer under death so we can choose life.

> Like the rest, we were by nature objects of wrath. But because of his great love for us, God, who is rich in mercy, made us alive with Christ even when we were dead in transgressions – it is by grace you have been saved.
> (Ephesians 2:3-5)

But as a child I didn't know this. I began to take on the role of protector towards my brother and sister. I took the brunt of things and tried to keep them out of the way. I'm not really sure what sort of dynamic sets itself up to do that at around three years old, which was when my brother was born. But there was something in me that just felt like I had to try to prevent this tiny little one from going through what I was going through. And so from the age of three, I tried to protect my brother, and then later my sister too.

And I thought that this life, my life, was normal. Some people can't understand that, but it never occurred to me as a young adult that my life wasn't normal. I never philosophised about life or envisioned what I might do as an adult; every day was a survival test – get through it and go to sleep at night and get up and get through it all over again.

I didn't always go to school as a child. Mother used to keep me home a lot, either doing chores or drawing me into her silly fantasies. In those days there were outside toilets or 'outbuildings' for keeping the coal and stuff. If my mother thought that anyone was going to be around, or was going to notice that I wasn't in school, she'd lock me in there. Or she'd just lock me in there because she didn't want me around. At the end of the school day she'd let me out. She didn't do it with the others and she didn't want other people to know that she was doing it. Our cottage faced on to a busy main trunk road with the 'coal store' attached to the side; no one knew I was in there, no one knew that she did that to me; that she locked me up in the coal store.

Yet, however unsafe that was for a child, to me it felt like a safe place, a place where I wasn't being shouted at, wasn't being beaten, and where I could just rest for a while. I became adept at contriving to be locked up, to find my safe place, and as an adult I became adept at pulling back into dissociating in any situation that felt threatening. I would find my safe place by 'switching off' and retreating into myself to survive what I couldn't cope with – and that was always to do with people; speaking to them, interacting with them. People were not to be trusted; people were frightening. I didn't consciously decide to do this, it was an automatic conditioned response, a way of my brain helping me survive at the time, causing me to think being *Nemo* and becoming invisible was the safest place to be. Now, like my grandfather, I hid in the nonentity of my existence.

At the end of a school day, the routine was that either I'd be brought out from where I'd been locked in or I came home from school if I'd actually been there, and the first thing I would do was to try to get in the house, because Mother would invariably be out. It was easy back then; there were windows that could be lifted up and people sometimes didn't lock the door – it wasn't like it is now in terms of tight security. Sometimes my brother would climb in through a window. Once I'd managed to get in the house, I'd start doing all the chores and various things to look after my brother and sister, and I'd do them all as fast as I could before Father came home.

I can remember an instance when I was around eight years old. We were all in the house except for Father, as he was at work. Mother had decided that she was going out so she'd put on all of her finery and was heading off. My sister was two years old and was crying because she wanted her mum. I had to literally hold her down to stop her from getting to my mother who was leaving the house and then console her after my mother had gone. Then I was left to look after her all on my own – at the age of eight. I don't know when I started babysitting my siblings, but I can remember it was at least from eight because that's when we moved house and we were no longer next door to my grandparents.

The general environment I lived in during this time was just one of fear, total fear; fear of Father and fear of Mother. Mother just had a sort of power over me, somehow. She never really hit me, but she would play the mind games and do the rituals that in many ways affected me far more than the things that my father did, because they affected my mind and the way that I thought about myself. For example, she would have an hour-long ritual every morning. She would sit me on the bed and she would sit facing me, then she would say to me for an hour, one hour timed exactly: 'You're mental, you, you need a doctor.' Again and again she would repeat it, over and over for the whole hour.

That's all she said. Every day for one hour in the morning: get up, get dressed, before school, before chores – this ritual. Over and over again. Sometimes when she lost her temper with me, she would say, 'Remember, you're mental, you need a doctor, you need to be in the asylum.' There was a local mental health institution that originally had been known as a 'lunatic asylum', so that's what she was referring to. I can't remember when that ritual started. It started as far back as I've got memories.

Much later in life when my mother was in a nursing home having then developed dementia, she would sometimes hide under the sheets crying. When I asked her what was wrong she said, 'They keep telling me I'm mental and need a doctor.' (Of course, none of the nursing staff had said such things.) I had discovered a bit more about her background by then and the first time I heard her say this I realised then that these words had been said to her when she was a child. How the work of the enemy can continue down a family line to wreck the lives of so many.

I didn't fully understand what those words meant when I heard them as a child, except that they told me I was different; that I wasn't 'right' and that there was something odd about me. The misuse of words like this can bind us up in a way that can affect our whole life. Such words became embedded within me, along with other things that were constantly said such as 'You're stupid', 'You're useless', 'You're a waste of space', 'You don't belong'. Eventually these things became powerful strongholds that ruled the way I saw myself and behaved.

And then, on top of that, there was school life. As I mentioned before, Mother didn't look after us and even though I thought I was helping to look after my brother and sister, being a child myself, I obviously didn't know how to properly look after children. So, we smelled because we didn't get bathed properly and we very regularly had head lice – every time the 'nit nurse' came to school, we had them! I remember that at least on one occasion I also had scabies. We looked a mess and my mother subjected all of us to her own weird haircuts. So, our family became renowned in the town – it was a very close-knit community back then and everybody knew everybody. And everyone knew my family and I was from 'that family'.

Then there were our clothes. Mother was a very proud woman. Part of being narcissistic often means that you can be very haughty and have a very high opinion of yourself, and she was like that. She wouldn't accept clothes from people around her. I remember once the mother of a classmate at school gave me a bag of clothes that her older daughter had grown out of; there was a lovely green cardigan in there that would have been so warm and soft to wear, but my mother was livid – she made me take them all back. It all added to the inner sense that I should not have anything, 'I am not good enough'.

At that time there were places, which were a bit like going to the Salvation Army, where one could go to get an outfit. We would be taken there, into this really dark, dank basement room and it would be full of different clothes; racks of women's, men's and various children's garments. That's where Mother would take us all to get our clothes, so nothing ever fitted properly and it left us wide open to being bullied at school, all three of us. I was very severely bullied at school right from the start. So, all of these factors in combination made me convinced that I was indeed 'odd' and 'mental' and 'didn't belong'.

The other thing was that I didn't talk. I was a selective mute until I was thirteen years old. When I was alone with my brother and sister I talked to them a little bit, but it didn't happen with anyone else except them. When I was seven or eight years old, because I didn't talk and because I was still wetting the bed, Mother took me to see the doctor and said, 'She doesn't talk to us and she still wets the bed every night. What's wrong with her?' But she never added, 'Oh, and we beat her up regularly.'

So around the age of nine I was sent to what was then called the Child Guidance Clinic. I have vague memories of going there; a place that was silent with big, squeaky, highly polished floors. I went a few times and was given a shape sorter and told to put the shapes in. I remember thinking 'Do they really think I can't do this?' because I knew that it was a baby's toy. But they obviously thought that I couldn't do it. Sometimes I was given two pictures that were wildly dissimilar and asked to point out the differences. I don't know exactly what they concluded, but they did discover that I'd got a problem with my bladder and kidneys that was causing the wet bed issue. In later childhood there were therefore a lot of hospital appointments to do with trying to sort that out.

I was a sickly child with aches and pains all the time, quite apart from the sick feeling of tension and anxiety permanently in the pit of my stomach, but I hated being ill; being ill meant being unable to do the chores and that made Mother angry and Father lose his temper. Mother would just shut me in the bedroom all day and push a tray around the door from time to time with a cup of weak tea and a few plain biscuits on it. This just added to the sense of loneliness and uselessness I felt, but at that time I could not have identified those feelings, they were just locked inside under the fear.

The eventual conclusion of many of the doctors was that there was no hope of seeing me achieve anything or grow up to hold down a job. I was written off as a disassociated 'hopeless case', a 'mentally defective' child.

But today I now know that there are no 'hopeless cases' – there are only those who have no hope.

At school, because I didn't speak, looked a mess, smelled, probably had nits and came from 'that family', I used to attract derision and all the worst from the bullies. The other kids would sometimes break my glasses so I wouldn't be able to see at all. I have a few eye problems which meant as a child I wore a pair of round National Health spectacles and a plaster over one of the eyepieces all the time. I didn't tell my parents what happened at school because I just didn't talk, but if some of the bullies had taken my specs and broken them and I went home with broken glasses, I would just end up getting beaten at home as well.

Beaten at school, beaten at home; life became one of simple survival. I would try to get through a school day without anything untoward happening that would be discovered at home, and then try to get home safely and then try to do as much at home as I could to try to stop the worst from happening. I suppose I was on a mission that was doomed to fail because actually I couldn't, could I – I couldn't stop it all happening? So I lived on the edge of my seat all the time, always screwed up inside.

In primary school there were class grades depending on how well the pupils did. I was put with the worst of the worst, the pupils they couldn't do anything with, either because of their behaviour or because they weren't capable. The overall opinion of me was that I wasn't capable of achieving anything or learning much. However, as long as I sat in a corner drawing, which was what I did like to do, they were happy to let me get on and do that because they just thought that I wasn't equipped for doing anything else and it was easy for them to leave me like that. So, in primary and junior school I was mostly ignored, and because I was just as frightened of the teachers as I was of my parents, I never did anything out of line. I just sat quietly in a corner with a whole load of coloured pencils. That summed up my existence.

So back at my grandparents' house, listening to my grandfather's stories of his life, I was already beginning to relate to the whole 'I'm a nobody' idea. I started to think, 'Yes, I'm a nobody as well.' I really cared for my grandfather; I really cared for them all, as odd as it sounds. There was a strange kind of dichotomy that set itself up in me; a loyalty to my family because they were all I knew, and at the same time a helpless despair that this was my family, whilst still seeing it as normal family life.

I think my father, in a funny sort of way, did actually care about me because I do have a few recollections of occasions when, after he'd beaten me very badly and then calmed down, he'd sometimes sit with me in quietness as if he was remorseful of what had just happened.

Most of the people around, including our neighbours, no doubt suspected what was going on. Recently, I had a chance meeting with a lady who had been in school at the same time as me. We hadn't met since schooldays but she told me she had wondered a lot over the years what had become of me because, as she said, 'We all knew what was going on.' But people didn't do anything back then. If there were systems or processes that could potentially intervene, I don't know how active they were; they certainly weren't active for us. Things just didn't happen in those days to the same degree that they happen now. No one was looking out for us, no one protected us. Even if they did suspect something was amiss, people just wouldn't, or didn't, do anything. And I couldn't talk to them anyway.

Life at that time was therefore simply about survival from one day to the next; I was unable to communicate well, generally disassociated and withdrawn, and switched off emotionally. If I was asked in later life 'How did you get on with Mum and Dad?' I always answered, 'Fine.' I had no concept that things actually weren't fine; being unable to experience the emotion of joy or happiness, to feel anything good, or make my own choices.

A person doesn't always realise things are not fine, or not normal, when they've had no other experience nor seen anything different to their own situation. Even when another family member began to sexually abuse me it was just another normal part of life. That particular phase lasted until I was about fourteen years old. I don't remember when it began, exactly, but it was before I was seven.

These kinds of experiences can leave us feeling unclean, dirty, like soiled goods, and it becomes like a bad, guilty secret filling us with shame. The thing about guilt is it can be associated with something we've done (or perceived we have done), but shame is something else. Shame invades the thinking about who we are. Shame hides itself and pervades the whole being, often with no real association to any particular action, and is therefore so hard to shake off. But we can come through to the place of forgetting the shame of our youth and instead know a 'double portion' of joy in God (Isaiah 54:4; 61:7).

As Christians, we have been 'rescued' from the authority of the enemy, the darkness of his dominion. The enemy, Satan, wants to keep us in darkness so he uses fears, rational or irrational – fears of other people, the fear of man (a snare), fear of being hurt, manipulated, controlled, rejected, persecuted, humiliated etc. All the things which human beings can do to their fellow humans. The enemy uses guilt or shame, whether it is as a result of something we have done or not.

These kinds of things can bind us up just as much as torment by any demon can; they bring their own form of torment.

Isaiah 61:1-3 says:

> The Spirit of the Sovereign LORD is on me, because the LORD has anointed me to proclaim good news to the poor. He has sent me to bind up the broken-hearted, to proclaim freedom for the captives and release from darkness for the prisoners, to proclaim the year of the LORD's favour and the day of vengeance of our God, to comfort all who mourn, and provide for those who grieve in Zion – to bestow on them a crown of beauty instead of ashes, the oil of joy instead of mourning, and a garment of praise instead of a spirit of despair. They will be called oaks of righteousness, a planting of the LORD for the display of his splendour.

God gives us a 'great exchange', all that is held under the authority of Satan is set free and brought into God's great kingdom under His supreme authority. Colossians 1:13 says, 'For he has rescued us from the dominion of darkness and brought us into the kingdom of the Son he loves' (from one lesser authority to another higher authority). It is therefore important that we look at the choices we make in life that enable us to live more and more in His kingdom instead of being dominated by sin and fear.

Chapter Three: *Nemo* is Formed

I never had any plans about 'when I grow up' because I just never thought about the future. I also didn't remember having any sense of fond memories of 'what happened yesterday' during that part of my life. Since then, and with a lot of healing, I have ended up remembering the odd nice time with my grandfather, but back then it was like I wasn't able to hold on to any happiness that took place because so many bad things had and were happening. The only thing I was focused on was: 'How can I get through today?'

My parents were not churchgoers, neither were my grandparents, but my parents for some reason had me christened shortly after I was born. I still don't know why, because my brother and sister were never christened. Until recently I never knew where my christening happened.

One of our neighbours used to look out for me a bit and when I was born she had given a little book, Cambridge *Picture, Prayer and Hymns,*[1] to my parents for me for my christening. I don't recall at what point I started knowing this was *my* book and I don't know at what point I started looking at it, but it was what it said – pictures, prayers and hymns! There were bits and pieces that I looked at in the written text, but it had colour pictures in it and, as a child, those colour pictures were all that mattered. There was one particular picture that stood out from them all. It was a picture of a man and to me that book was all about the 'Man in the Picture'. That man was Jesus, although as a child, I didn't actually know anything about Him, nor have any concept of Jesus or God.

---

[1] *Cambridge Picture Prayer and Hymns* (Book of Common Prayer with Hymns Ancient and Modern) (Cambridge/London: Cambridge University Press/William Clowes & Sons, Cambridge, 1939).

I never heard anything Jesus-related, but somehow when I'd been beaten and felt all horrible inside, looking at that picture made me feel better. So, every time I got beaten, I'd go and curl up in my bed, get the little book out and just stare at that picture.

On one particular occasion when I was about eight or nine, I'd had a particularly bad beating and I didn't know where I was at all. I curled up into bed, got out the book and was just staring at that picture as usual. And then, as unbelievable as it may sound, it seemed as if the man just came straight out of that page. You may argue that it was some kind of hallucination because of the severity of the beating, and I'm not too worried what anybody's view on that is. I did have some bad beatings that affected my ability to think straight, but to me in that moment He was absolutely real. And He said to me, 'Don't worry. One day you'll find your real Father.'

So every beating I ever had after that, I would get out my little book and I would look at that picture and I'd think, 'One day I'm going to find my real Father.' Over the years as I got a bit older and I read Charles Dickens' Oliver and other stories where the badly treated orphan finds their real family, I slowly took on the idea that I'd been adopted. I therefore believed that one day I'd find my real Father, or rather, that he'd come and find me. That's what kept me going and fighting for survival until I was fifteen years old; the thought that 'One day I'll find my real Father'. I don't know how I'd have got through those years if I hadn't had that thought to hold on to.

When I reached the end of junior school years I, like everyone else, had to take the Eleven Plus, an educational marker at the time to decide on your eventual academic potential. I obviously failed mine because I hadn't learned anything. I could, however, read and write far more than anyone knew, and this was how *Nemo* became fully formed within me.

Father, being the clever man that he was, was a book lover and often went to the library to borrow books. I think he lost himself in them and I kind of followed in his footsteps with this. Even though at school I wasn't being given anything to read, at home I was reading any and every book that I could lay my hands on. I read and read and read; I just escaped into books.

Father had entire collections of books from his own growing-up years. For instance, he had an entire collection of Arthur Ransome's *Swallows and Amazons* stories about children playing on boats, and a lot of the classic Dickens stories. But he also had books by Jules Verne. In one of Jules Verne's books, *20,000 Leagues Under the Sea*, one of the principal characters is called Captain Nemo. He's called Nemo because he's been exiled from his original home and he's wandering around in this boat like a nobody without any identity. No one knows who he is and where he's from; he hides and he doesn't want to be seen. When I read that book, I didn't so much identify with what the character got up to, but I immediately identified with the concept of 'nemo'. I was about nine when this happened and I just thought, 'That's me, my name is *Nemo*.' I got a dictionary out and looked it up and found out that *Nemo* in Latin means 'no man, nobody.'

And I just said to myself, 'My name is *Nemo*. I am a nobody. I do not have an identity. I must hide and never be seen or heard.' I didn't realise at the time but I had just spoken a curse over myself that would take years to break free from.

But I couldn't always hide away and read. I remember having some really scary times. On one occasion at school the bullies managed to get hold of me; two of them grabbed my legs and two of them grabbed my arms. They picked me up and swung me back and forth between the four of them and then, all of a sudden, they let me go… over a six-foot-high wall, *smack!* onto the ground, right on top of a pile of bricks. It took the breath out of me. I remember lying down looking at the sky – it was a lovely blue with fluffy white clouds going past. I wasn't breathing because the impact had winded me so much. Then everything became really, really peaceful.

I thought, 'It's alright to die, it's quite nice, this.' And I felt the attraction of leaving this world and its suffering behind for good, and the feeling of wanting that to happen entered in and was to became another big part of the battle. But then, all of a sudden, I was gasping for breath as the automatic nature of the body forced my lungs into action again.

Things like that happened to me regularly. Sometimes the bullies would get me in the toilet block outside the PE (physical education) field. They would stuff my face down the toilet bowl until I gagged and choked on the toilet water. I'd then go home but I couldn't let them know about it there because I might get even more of the same as, once again, my spectacles would be broken. Oh, the number of pairs of spectacles that I got through in those years! But all the while I hung on to this idea that my adoptive family would one day find me.

I think my grandfather's story somehow had engrained itself in me as well, because of the fact that we hadn't taken on my grandfather's legal name. When father had joined the army, he joined with his legal name, even though both he and my uncle were actually known by the name of the family who'd raised my grandfather. This sometimes made things tricky because, for example, when the sergeant major shouted out his orders, my father didn't always respond quickly enough, as he wasn't used to hearing that name. So, he often got into bother! In the end, he changed his name by deed poll to the name he had been known by growing up, although my uncle always kept to his original birth name. I suppose that somehow in my childlike brain I wove a connection between this story and the man who'd come out from the page and I somehow decided that my real 'legal' family would one day find me and everything would be alright and then I would no longer be with this man and woman who did all this stuff to me.

In the meantime, I just carried on in life and I was always OK as long as nobody spoke to me and everyone ignored me and I could stay in the background and be *Nemo*. I just kept out of the way because I was still just so frightened of everyone. I was especially frightened of people in any kind of authority. As an older teenager I would never go to the doctor unless I could help it because I was also frightened of him, and I didn't like going to the bank because I was scared of all the people behind the bank screens. I was afraid of just about everybody.

I started secondary school at about eleven or twelve years old and was ranked at the bottom of the bottom class, academically speaking. This particular class was a mixed bag of pupils, like myself, who had difficulties one way or the other. There were probably autistic children (though as yet autism was not readily spoken of or recognised) in that class. And then on the other end of the scale there were kids that may have been very, very capable but had behavioural problems. We'd all be together mixed up in the same class. Some of the worst bullies in the school ended up being in the same class as me because of their behavioural problems, so it just made for an even more difficult environment.

Things changed a bit in the second year when I was thirteen years old. My form teacher was also the English teacher and on one occasion he set an assignment for all his pupils, which was to write a poem. I had a go and my teacher said that my poem was very good and slowly he began to realise through the English lessons that there was actually more 'under my bonnet', as he called it, than had originally been supposed. He began to ask me to write more poems for him, which I did. He then started asking me about the poems.

I don't remember what made this particular day any different, maybe it was his persistent encouragement, but on one occasion I actually ended up responding to him and just answered his question. So, he broke through the mutism and got me talking, although I still had very few words and was very stunted in my verbal interaction.

I ended up being in his form for another year. For two consecutive years I was in the same form, and I had the same teacher for English lessons right up until my last year in school. He actually shouldn't have had the class that I was in originally because he was supposed to teach the children going on to do A-levels. However, he ended up temporarily covering someone that year, which is why he got the people like me. So, when in the second year he was my teacher again, because of his input and encouragement, I went from the ranking of bottom of the bottom class, to being among those ranked at the top of the top class. God used that teacher to help me. I have no idea whether he was a Christian but he was compassionate and caring.

Never underestimate the power of your care and compassion to bring healing, hope and change to the life of others. The smallest gesture, such as the lady giving me the book on my christening, and this teacher, with his care and persistent encouragement, meant my life was impacted in a major way. We can impact the lives of others far more than we realise as we reach out to them with care and compassion, even in small ways.

Eventually, the teachers began to realise that I did actually have potential, and as a result they began to put me in the classes where I was possibly on track to do A-levels. I think that I just woke up to the fact that I was supposed to be learning. But I also think it was because I was afraid of the teachers; I did my homework because I always did what was asked of me. I never queried things, or questioned things, or shied away from doing what was asked of me because I was frightened of the consequences if I didn't do what I was asked to do. To me, I never had any choice in anything; or rather, I never had the sense that I had the choice. So, if my teacher said to the pupils, 'Choose a book from this list,' I couldn't do that. He would have to give me a book title, or I would simply work down the list.

At home, in reading the books around me, I had devised ways of avoiding choice. I would put them all in date order or find some other way of ordering them so that the choice was made for me. I couldn't actually make a choice even if I wanted to, because I just didn't know how to choose.

Chapter Four: Ruled by Poverty

At fifteen, I had managed to survive life so far when two significant things happened. I was now in my last year at school and having to do extra lessons in everything; from French and geography, to English and science. For English class, one of the things I had to do was a project about the locality. I can't remember what the main point of the project was supposed to be, but mine meant investigating all the local ghost stories and the whole question of: 'Is there such a thing as the supernatural?' and 'Are there such things as ghosts and do they really haunt this town?'

I had to spend a year doing this project and I'd been doing it for nine months. The English teacher had said that what I'd done so far was good and that I should get a really good mark for it. I was in the last three months of this project and had just done some more work on it before going to bed one evening. Then, all of a sudden, I found myself wide awake in the middle of the night, full of fear with a particularl story of a haunting on my mind. Then I heard Him, the Man in the Picture, and He said, 'No more'. Two words: 'No more.' It was almost as if my hair stood on end, it was so frightening. And I knew that I knew, that I knew, that I could not do this project anymore, that this voice had to be obeyed. I'd got into Edgar Allan Poe stories and other supernatural thriller writers; not just children's stories but adult fear novels, and I had been soaking it all up. When I heard this 'No more' I just knew that I shouldn't delve into or read any of these things anymore. I didn't know why, but I just knew I wasn't allowed to carry on with it.

I went to school the next day and I told my teacher that I couldn't do this project anymore. He said, 'You can't stop that now!' and tried to talk me into carrying on, but I just said, 'No, I'm not doing it anymore.' I'd made my first conscious choice because of the directive of the Man in the Picture; I was doing as I had been told to do. Later in life I realised that it was the hand of God stopping me from going down a route that the enemy had tried to take me down.

So I suddenly changed tack and was given another project about the types of houses in the area. I got a very average mark because I did it all in a bit of a rush at the last minute! My teacher never understood why I stopped doing the first project, because I never told him. I thought that nobody would understand, because I never wanted to tell anybody about the Man in the Picture because I knew I was 'odd' and also, by this time, at fifteen, I knew what 'going into the asylum' meant; it meant that you were mad. So, somewhere inside myself I thought that's really what my problem was: 'I'm not "right", I'm mad.'

The other thing that happened took place only weeks after the 'No more' experience. I had to take my birth certificate to school as part of the whole process of leaving school which, by the way, I did; I left school just before I was sixteen as Father would not let me go to university (I did that later in life). School sent him a letter saying that they wanted to send me to grammar school to do A-levels and then on to university. But to him it wasn't an option for me: 'No, you're not doing that.' He'd never been given the chance, so why should I be given a chance? He had to go out to earn a living to help the family keep going, so now I had to go out and earn a living to help keep the family going.

So I had now reached the point where I was leaving school to get a job and had to take in my birth certificate. And for the first time ever, I saw it. I saw that I wasn't adopted after all.

That's when my world caved in. As far as I was now concerned, there was nothing to keep going for anymore, there was no 'real Father' to find and the Man in the Picture had lied to me. I plunged into a black, suicidal depression. I remembered the feeling when I'd been thrown over the wall and I began to think about dying and killing myself all the time. I just didn't want to be alive. I, *Nemo*, the nobody that had no identity, now didn't even want to have an existence.

However, the whole problem about not being able to choose meant that I was unable to make the clear choice to commit suicide, even though I was plagued with thoughts of it all the time. I was trying to get to a place of deciding to do it, but I was also frightened to do it. Faced with choices, I went into this terrible fear that I'd make the wrong choice, whatever that choice might be – it didn't matter how big or small it was.

Between the ages of fifteen and eighteen was one big unhappy blur for me as I simply tried to keep myself going, surviving, for just one more day. I was in my first job but still I just saw my life as existing through to the end of every day. Life at home was still the same. I didn't like the working environment any more than school; people were still bullies, but just in a slightly more refined, adult way. I was still frightened of everyone. I still couldn't speak up for myself or answer anyone back. I couldn't maintain a conversation and if people tried to talk to me I would try to respond, but it was so restricted to one word answers that they gave up trying! I just wanted to be left in a corner at my desk to get on with my work. You know when you get tense and get 'butterflies'? I didn't realise it, but that's how I was 100 per cent of the time; tense and full of anxieties. I didn't know what the word 'relax' meant. It was like I had an elastic band right down through the core of my being, stretched very, very tight. All the time.

Childhood fears subtly refine themselves into our adult being. My fear of my parents, the bullies at school and so on, had grown into a fear of people in authority such as doctors, bank managers and later even church leaders. My fear of being shut into dark, damp places immobilised me from being able to access the cellar in our marital home as an adult, and my fear of what would happen if I didn't do the chores morphed into a fear of being ill and thereby being unable to do what I *should* be doing to serve and keep everyone around me happy. The loneliness and depression just grew stronger and stronger, trapping me into its prison and swallowing me up.

There were various conditions that I'd been labelled as having, medically speaking. I can't remember all of the names but one of them was about having a dysfunctional personality, 'dissociative identity disorder'. It was the one I remember the most because it was the one that I struggled with the longest. As part of the condition, I couldn't hold on to the sense of good things. If something good happened, I didn't even think, 'It's not meant for me' because it simply would not occur to me that anything good *could* happen for me, it would just bypass me. I'd learned to never expect anything good and I'd been conditioned to believe I shouldn't have anything. When I did get a job, I would hand my weekly wage packet over to Mother, but if I wanted a magazine or a chocolate bar I practically had to beg for it and risk the mind games all over again. So, I stopped asking, I went without. I was undeserving of anything good, that's what I believed.

These types of things create a poverty of spirit that roots itself deep inside, and it's not so much about finances, more that one's inner being embraces the expectation of poverty and lack. Even those with a healthy bank balance could be driven by poverty of spirit; afraid to give too much in case next week there is a need for what is currently in the bank. Or even maybe a person could have a lot of money and give away a lot yet still be driven to make money in order to stave off the poverty they unconsciously perceive to be their lot if they stop. I was yet to learn that Father God is an abundant God who expels poverty of spirit, taking us on adventures whereby we learn that He meets all our needs according to His riches (Philippians 4:19) and is totally able to provide for all our tomorrows, whatever our bank balance.

But at that time in my life it certainly felt as though nothing good ever happened. It was almost like I felt only bad things were meant to happen to me. So, I had absolutely no positive emotion attached to anything. I didn't even get or feel upset. Having a dissociative personality meant that I was totally removed from that, so I didn't feel hurt and upset and I didn't cry, because I couldn't feel like crying. There was a kind of pain somewhere deep inside me, but the abiding emotion I experienced was fear. And that was my life stretched out before me, although I had never looked at it like that before because I'd never thought about my future. I had always thought, 'One day my real Father is coming', but now of course my real Father was not coming, I already lived with him. I just decided that I really must be mad to have believed that for all those years. Therefore, when Mother was saying (still) every day for exactly an hour, 'You're mental, you, you need a doctor' that now made sense to me. Of course I was 'mental', of course I needed a doctor. She drilled that into me for years and years: 'You're mental, you, you need a doctor,' right up until the day I left home and even on the day of my wedding.

Chapter Five:
Jesus: The Man in the Picture

The things which are repeatedly said to us can settle into us so deeply that we never question them. I believed what I was told; I based all my conclusions about myself on what was said and done to me. I was odd, had mental health issues, was a hopeless case that would never achieve anything, should never have anything, worthless and a nobody, I was *Nemo* and now I needed to die. But I was listening to the wrong voice; I was listening to an enemy who simply wanted to rob and destroy. But, of course, I didn't know that then; I was like a lost sheep straying into a dangerous road. I needed to listen to another voice, the voice of a good shepherd who leads His flock away from danger.

Jesus said:

> Very truly I tell you, I am the gate for the sheep … I am the gate; whoever enters through me will be saved. They will come in and go out, and find pasture. The thief [the enemy, Satan, the devil] comes only to steal and kill and destroy; I have come that they may have life and have it to the full. I am the good shepherd. The good shepherd lays down his life for the sheep.
> (John 10:7,9-11)

Too many of us do not recognise that we are listening to the wrong voice. There are many voices clamouring for our attention; for example, advertising is designed to 'speak' to us and subtly entice us to buy a particular product, people give us messages in their body language that speak to us of when they are upset with us or pleased with us – but for the purposes of my point here, there are three voices we could listen to:

1) God's voice
2) Our own voice
3) The enemy's voice.

There are examples of those who heard God's audible voice; Moses hearing God at the bush on Mount Horeb (Exodus 3), Elijah hearing God at the cave (1 Kings 19), or Samuel hearing God as he lay in the temple (1 Samuel 3). But we can also learn to recognise our own voice or running commentary within ourselves; it is shaped by our personality and our experiences. Typically we hear things like: 'I can't do that. I'm not that type of person!' Who says? What does God say?

Then, of course, there is the voice of the enemy who will try to pull us back, accuse us, rob us in some way. He will often agree with my negative assessment of myself adding in his 'Yes, you'd be no good at that' to whatever I'm telling myself. And typically we tend to endorse what others have negatively said about us by repeating those things to ourselves, and we believe those things to be true because they are familiar to us. The enemy robs us and we so often rob ourselves by adding our own voice in agreement with him. Anything that assails you with accusation, criticism, despair, negativity, or any other thing which robs you is from the voice of an enemy. He 'prowls around like a roaring lion' (1 Peter 5:8) seeking any opportunity to 'steal and kill and destroy' (John 10:10).

The year I turned eighteen, things at home were just the same, even though I was older. I was still earnestly doing the chores, sustaining regular beatings and enduring the daily rituals. The only thing that stopped was getting locked up in the outbuildings. The only reason that stopped was because when I was about sixteen, we went out to it one day and the wind caught the door and the key hit my mother's head and cut her. She never did it again after that. So, I stopped getting locked in there.

During this time, I started the beginnings of what could have been a rebellion, although it never got that far. I had decided that my parents could not possibly physically hurt me more than they already had unless they killed me, and if they killed me then that wouldn't matter because then they would have done it for me. As a result, I stopped caring about my parents' reactions to things. Although I was still afraid of them on one level, at another level, because I didn't want to exist, I didn't care about their wrath anymore. I had lost the fear of no longer existing; I had lost the fear of death.

One of the things my parents had said that I couldn't do was to go to the local youth club or, indeed, any other clubs. Well, I didn't care about that prohibition anymore, so I fell into a pattern of going to the clubs in the town centre with a group of girls on a Sunday night. They weren't friends as such, they were just a gang I went with. I was actually just a foil; I was the one they made fun of while we were out. But they were people to go out with, nevertheless, and I knew they were using me: I never got drunk so I was the one who made sure we got a taxi home.

After a night out, we'd all share a taxi to get home because it was about ten miles away from where we lived. So, that's what my Sunday nights became like; I'd go out to the clubs, finish at about 2 or 3 a.m., get our taxi home and then get to bed and have about two hours sleep before I had to get up again for work. The others would get really drunk but I never drank too much because I didn't particularly like alcohol. I actually couldn't see the point of getting drunk and I couldn't see the point of doing drugs. I smoked a bit, but only normal cigarettes and simply because it gave me something to do when I was fed up sitting by myself whilst the other girls were all trying to 'get off' with the lads. I just couldn't see the point of all of these things that everyone seemed to be trying at that time. Everything just seemed empty.

When I turned eighteen years old, my parents said, 'Well, don't think you're getting any special presents just because your eighteen, because that's supposed to be when you're twenty-one.' I didn't get any special presents anyway, so that didn't bother me. When I found out that I could vote at eighteen, I didn't have a clue about the political system. I really had no idea. At one point when one of the elections came up, my father said, 'Right, we're going to vote and everybody's name is going to be on this slip and you're going to put a cross on this name.' He basically told me who to vote for. So, I obediently put a cross against the appropriate name and I put it in the box. When I came outside Father asked me whether I'd voted for the person he'd told me to vote for and I said, 'Yes.' However, on the way back down the hill, I wondered why and thought, 'Why am I always doing what he tells me? Why will I never do anything unless somebody's told me to do it?'

It was the first time I actually questioned my actions and why I always did what someone else had told me to do. But then, just having that very thought filled me with fear. In that moment I felt like I couldn't face any more of life doing everything everybody said and not knowing how to do anything for myself. I did, of course, in one sense know how to do a lot, in terms of physical chores, but it was always within a confined environment of being told what to do and with the threat of abuse. So, for instance, it was my job to light the fire every morning but that didn't involve any choice. You knew what you had to do and you did it. So, after thinking, 'I can't face going on another day like this, being told what to do,' I thought, 'I'm going to commit suicide.'

However, because that in itself was a choice and needed preparation, I needed to have a plan, and adjust myself to the idea. I thought, 'I'm going to pick a date on the calendar. It's going to be a Sunday night, because what I'm going to do is to save up tablets, anything I can buy, like headache tablets, and then I'll go out with the girls, I'll drink more alcohol than normal, then I'll come home and I'll swallow everything that I've saved up and then I'll go to bed and never wake up. Then I really won't exist anymore.' I was listening to my own voice, big time!

So that was the 'grand plan', as I thought of it. I can't remember when I formulated it all, but the planned suicide date was the first Sunday in July that year. It was just a date I'd picked by closing my eyes and pointing at the calendar; there was no significance to that date, or at least I didn't think there was. It was just about six weeks or so hence and I thought that would be enough time to save up my pills and potions and build up the courage to do the act. So, that's what I did; I started saving up various medications. And strangely enough, having got this grand plan in my head that no one knew about, I actually rallied a bit and it kept me going in those interim weeks. So, I carried on with life as usual until it got to that Sunday.

On the night itself, the plan was to go out with the girls to the nightclub as per a usual Sunday. However, I first need to set the scene for you: this was before the 'punk' era, but I'd come up with 'punk' in my own way. I had every fingernail painted in a different colour; I had weird shades of various coloured make-up on my face (not just my eyes, but all over my face), along with thick layers of eyeliner and mascara (because that's what one did in the 1960s and 70s). And then I was wearing a suede miniskirt that only just covered my rear – I was six feet tall and my legs are about four feet long (OK, I exaggerate!). I certainly looked strange and had no dress sense whatsoever.

So I got ready that evening in this manner and went to call on one of the girls. However, that night it turned out that she wasn't able to come out because some of her relatives had just turned up. So, I went somewhere else, but the next girl was ill and wasn't able to come out either. I then went somewhere else, but this particular girl had got into trouble in a big way and was not allowed out. One by one, everyone dropped out and none of the usual gang ended up being able to go out. This was a severe hitch in my plan! Right at the start, this shouldn't have happened – we went out every Sunday! Except for tonight, apparently.

So, I went back home. Mother and Father were watching television and my sister also happened to be around. For a number of months now, my sister had been going to what she called the 'coffee bar', which was held on the first Sunday of every month in a local church hall. Its purpose was to gather together young people from all the local churches in order to do something evangelistic. My sister had been attending this every month, even though she wasn't a Christian. Every month she'd say to me, 'Will you go to this coffee bar with me?' I think she'd been encouraged to try to take her friends along. Every month I'd say, 'No, why would I want to do that?' Why would I want to be seen out with a twelve-year-old when I was eighteen? Six years is a big gap when you're that age!

Anyway, that night I returned home and straightaway Mother exclaimed, 'What are you doing back?' I think she'd been getting used to me disappearing on Sunday nights and she didn't like the fact that I'd come home again. I replied, 'Well, nobody's going out so I'm not sure what to do.'

My sister then spoke up and said, 'I'm going out to the coffee bar, why don't you come with me?' to which I gave her my usual response, 'No, why would I want to do that?' But then my mother began having a go at me, saying, 'You never go anywhere with your sister. You don't care about anybody but yourself. You don't care about your sister!' I could see my father starting to get agitated and then Mother turned to him and continued, 'It's always the same, isn't it? She's no good for anything; she doesn't care about anybody but herself.'

I could feel the tension rising and I could tell that if I stuck around I'd end up with another beating. I had to get out so I decided that the better of two evils was to go to this coffee bar with my sister and get out of the way. I started walking with her and then instantly regretted it because she started chattering on and on about it, but I didn't know what else to do. I managed to reassure myself with the fact that after I'd got back from the coffee bar I'd take every pill I'd got and hope that that it would work anyway, even without any alcohol. And it probably would have done with all the stuff I'd managed to save up.

One of the things my sister had been telling me over the months was that there was a boy who went to the coffee bar that she thought

I knew. She described him with great detail but I had no idea who she was talking about. Anyway, we got to the venue, which belonged to a Methodist church, and as we walked through the door the first thing that happened was that a girl who I'd been at school with was there, in her full Salvation Army uniform (and remember, I'm in my miniskirt ready to go out clubbing with all my weird make-up on, so I blended in wonderfully!). She shouted across the room, 'What on earth are you doing here?'

I looked at her and thought, 'Well, if this is what's going to happen, then I'm going.'

I turned around to leave but my sister was in the doorway talking to a young man and saying, 'This is my sister – you know, who I was telling you about.' He looked at me and I looked at him; neither of us had ever seen each other before. But he started talking to me nevertheless and chatted away, and so I ended up being totally trapped in the doorway with this young man. And then the meeting started.

There was supposed to have been a Christian band, but they didn't turn up, so they'd asked the local Methodist minister (resplendent in all his Methodist robes) to come and do some kind of evangelistic talk. This was all very weird for me; I'd never been in a church before.

The meeting started. Well, one thing that I wasn't was impolite. Everyone had been told to sit down and so I felt obliged to sit down, because I always did what I was told. So, I sat down and the minister proceeded to say whatever he said. It was something about one man having a ticket to heaven and giving it to another man but the ticket didn't work for the other man, but I can't quite remember the story. He was basically giving a gospel presentation but it went totally over my head; I didn't understand a word of it, I didn't get it at all. I was just waiting to go home.

At the end of his talk, the minister said, 'We're all going to close our eyes and bow in prayer and then I'm going to ask you three times, if you want to become a Christian, stand up.' So, he began to do exactly that and began by saying, 'Let's all bow in prayer.' I had no idea what 'bow in prayer' meant, so I just looked at what everyone else was doing and just copied them by dipping my head down. As promised, he then asked the question, 'Does anybody want to become a Christian?'

When he gave his invitation the first time, I had a strange sensation in my whole body; it felt like somebody had switched on a magnet underneath my seat and this magnet started to pull me down into my seat. He then said a second time, 'Does anybody want to become a Christian?' and the sensation intensified; it felt like the magnetic pull became even stronger, as though I was going to go through the chair and through the floor and down to a lower level – it felt that powerful! When he said for a final time, 'I'm going to ask you a third time – does anybody want to become a Christian?', all of a sudden it was as if someone had instantly switched the power off from the magnet, with the result that I found myself catapulted out of my chair and flung straight onto my feet. I now found myself standing up, without having actually made any decision to stand up!

At that point in life I couldn't make a decision. I wouldn't have been able to have decided to become a Christian. I was catapulted onto my feet and this little voice inside me said, 'What are you doing this for?' Then the minister said, 'Right, you two [someone else had stood up too], follow me – we'll go into the vestry and I'll have a chat with you both.' So, I followed the minister, all the time thinking, 'What are you doing?' But it was as if I was on some kind of automatic pilot, unable to do anything else. I just had to follow the instructions.

So we went into a small room with the minister and he said to both of us, 'To be a Christian you have to repent of your sins and ask Jesus into your heart, so that's what we're going to do now. I'm going to say a prayer and you're going to say it too, one line at a time, after me.' So that's what we did. He said one line and we repeated it after him, and it kept going like that and all the while I was thinking, 'What are you doing?' I just wanted to go home! I had no idea why I was doing what I was doing, but I couldn't stop myself.

Then at the end of his prayer the minister said, 'Now you are a Christian. Go home, read your Bible every day and pray every day.' And then he added, 'Oh, and when you go out of this room and back into the hall, tell the friends that you've come with that you've become a Christian.' So, I went out of the room and back into the hall thinking, 'What are you doing?' with one thought, but then also with another thought remembering, 'Tell the friends you've come with.' But I hadn't come with any friends. Then I saw the boy who had been chatting to me earlier, Stuart, and thought, 'I know, I'll go and tell him,' but all the while at the same time thinking, 'What are you doing this for?'

'I have become a Christian!' I blurted out.

'Praise the Lord! Hallelujah!' Stuart replied in a most elated way. I thought his reaction was very weird. He then said, 'Do you want to come to a Bible study? All the young people get together on a Tuesday night.'

I looked at him quizzically, 'No, what would I want to do that for?'

'Well, because you've become a Christian,' he replied.

To which I said, 'Oh no, no, I don't want to do that, I can't do that.'

After that I went home thinking, 'What was that all about?'

When I got home, my sister went to bed straight away, but I just sat for a bit. I felt like a recording was going around and around in my head and I still felt a little as if I were on the automatic pilot: 'Read your Bible, read your Bible every day, read your Bible.' I thought, 'I don't know if there is a Bible in the house.' Then I remembered that when I first went into secondary school, every new pupil was given a Bible, and eventually I found it. It was an Authorized (King James) Version and I started reading it at page one. By the way, page one is not Genesis chapter 1, it's the beginning of an entire preamble! But

I started reading it at page one because that's how you read a book, isn't it?

It was now really late at night. I'm a very fast reader, so I read quite a lot and got through to Leviticus, to the bit about sores, and I thought, 'I have no idea what this means! Surely they didn't mean that I've got to read all of this, every day?' I got fed up eventually and closed the book. But as soon as I closed the Bible I then couldn't stop thinking, 'Pray every day, pray every day.' It was like the recording was on repeat. I thought, 'Well, I know, we did the Lord's Prayer at school.' So, I tried to remember bits of that and said the parts that I could remember.

When I'd said those parts I thought, 'I'm ready for bed!' It was about 3 a.m. by then. I still had all that weird make-up on and so I started to remove it. When I was in the process of taking it off my face, I suddenly thought, 'Christians probably shouldn't do this; plaster this stuff all over yourself.' So, I threw it all in the bin. Then I finished getting ready for bed and I got a cigarette out and my matches and then lit up. But then I thought, 'Christians probably shouldn't do this.' I put out my cigarette and threw those all in the bin too.

After I'd thrown them in the bin, I remembered the grand plan and thought, 'Right, this is it now, then.' I took time getting everything out of packets and got a big glass of water, but then I looked at the big pile of all the pills and thought, 'You know what, Christians probably shouldn't do this either.' And I flushed the whole lot down the toilet.

This all took place on the first Sunday in July, the year that I officially became an adult. I didn't realise until years later the significance of becoming a Christian on the first Sunday in July of my first adult year, but the lady who gave me that little book of prayers gave me that book for my christening which was on the first Sunday in July, the year I was born. I didn't discover this until my mother died, but it also turned out that I was christened in the same church building that I had become a Christian in.

So, in that moment, although I didn't realise this until many years later, that was the moment that I'd found my real Father. Or rather, He found me.

We often forget a simple truth when we're striving to be somebody or shrinking back into our nothingness. We forget that the Father chose us, we did not choose Him. Ephesians 1:4 says, 'For he [the Father] chose us in him [Jesus] before the creation of the world to be holy and blameless in his sight.' He chose us; to adopt us into His family, to make disciples out of us, to send us forth as His witnesses and to bear much fruit (John 15:16). To give us a voice.

He works in us to change us 'from one degree of glory to another' (2 Corinthians 3:18, ESV). I've heard people say, 'He loves me just as I am!' and yes, that's true, He does. But we're not meant to stay 'just as I am'. We are to allow His Spirit to work out His purpose for our lives, helping us to change as we learn to live with one another, to bear one another's burdens, to forgive one another and learn to walk alongside one another in love. As we grasp the truth of His Word, we are to let it fashion us and mould us into the new creation we are meant to be (2 Corinthians 5:17). He loved me just as I was, He loves me just as I am and He loves me just as I will be. I am a person who is in the transit of change.

Chapter Six: I Consecrated You Before You Were Born

After flushing all the tablets down the toilet, I then got into bed, still in this strange robotic place, and went to sleep. When I woke up the next morning, I felt completely different. I now knew for certain that the Man in the Picture was inside me, somehow. He was within me and outside of me all at the same time. I felt totally different, though nothing had changed and the depression hadn't gone. But I knew that my life was different and that I couldn't do the going out on Sundays anymore. And strangely, all of a sudden, I desperately, desperately wanted to get to the Tuesday Bible study! I didn't think that my sister went to it – she didn't – so I decided to try to find out where it was. My sister suggested that Stuart might know, but I didn't even know how to find Stuart. I honestly don't remember how she found out, but she did somehow and arranged for him to meet me and take me to the Bible study on the following Tuesday evening.

In that first week of my Christian life, the minister's instructions kept going around in my head: 'Read your Bible every day, pray every day.' I was naturally an avid reader because I was used to reading as an escape, and now I was being obedient to the minister. I stopped reading other books and was just reading my Bible; trying to understand it but not understanding it at all. I got to the prophets pretty quickly and I arrived at Jeremiah somewhere at the end of that first week. As I was reading Jeremiah, I read one particular part which felt like it 'stood out on stalks', as if it were in capitals and bold type:

> Before I formed thee in the belly I knew thee; and before thou camest forth out of the womb I sanctified [consecrated: ESV] thee, and I ordained thee a prophet unto the nations.
> (Jeremiah 1:5, AKJV)

Well, given that I'd decided that I was no man – 'I'm *Nemo*, I don't exist, I have no identity, no purpose, I shouldn't be here' – and because I was still fighting with this suicidal urge all the time, for that verse to effectively read 'before I formed you in the womb, before you were born, I had a purpose for you', that really went deep inside me. When I read that, something in me – although I didn't understand why – really did understand that to take your own life would be very wrong because of what it says: 'before you were born I consecrated you' (ESV).

The part that said, in the more modern NIV, 'I appointed you as a prophet to the nations' also really stood out. I really did take it in as this was what God was saying to me, but I didn't know what it meant. I didn't know what a prophet was. Then the next verse read, 'Then said I, Ah, Lord GOD! behold, I cannot speak: for I am a child' (Jeremiah 1:6, AKJV). I read it just at the point where I had begun to say exactly the same thing to God, 'But I can't speak!' I knew then that being a prophet must be something to do with speaking because in the text Jeremiah is saying, 'But I can't!' and I knew that I, too, was saying, 'But I can't.'

Then it says, in verse 7: 'But the LORD said unto me, Say not, I am a child' (or, as the ESV has it, 'a youth') – that was the other aspect that was relevant to me, because I was only eighteen. And then finally, this part really impacted me: 'for thou shalt go to all that I shall send thee, and whatsoever I command thee thou shalt speak. Be not afraid of their faces: for I am with thee to deliver thee, saith the LORD' (Jeremiah 1:7,8 AKJV).

So it was saying that everywhere God wanted me to go, I'd got to go, and everything He wanted me to say, I'd got to say and not to be afraid of people's faces, however afraid I was of people. The fear then kicked in again but now it was a fear of God: 'I've got to do this, because He's telling me to do it!' even though I didn't even know what it meant at this point. So, those four verses really stood out and I knew that God had spoken to me, even though I wouldn't have used that language. I never said, 'God has spoken to me' nor 'I've heard God say', I just experienced a heightened awareness of God's presence and felt that this was God speaking to me, the Man in the Picture again. That was the end of the first week after I'd become a Christian and that has stuck with me ever since and has never changed. This is my foremost commission in life.

There were also other things beginning to change in my life. About two weeks after becoming a Christian, which was also two weeks after I had met him, Stuart asked me to marry him. Apparently on the night that we met, he just knew from God that I was going to be his wife! Because of my upbringing and how that had led me to simply act out of obedience and to not have the ability to make a choice, when Stuart asked me to marry him, I saw it as if I had no choice. So, I just said 'yes', because 'Well, I've been asked, therefore I should'. At that point, I wasn't capable of feeling good feelings. I suppose I did love and care, which showed in the way that I looked after my siblings, but I didn't have any feelings of being loved. Neither did I know how to reciprocate any of those feelings. Even though those positive emotions were now being directed towards me, I could not experience them. So, the fact that Stuart asked me out and then asked me to marry him didn't mean that at that point I had any sense of feeling his love for me.

Nor did I have any sense of feeling God's love for me. At that point in my life I wouldn't have been able to have said, 'I feel God loves me' or that 'I feel Stuart loves me'. But that wasn't extraordinary because I hadn't had that feeling about anyone. So, when Stuart asked me to marry him, the correct answer was 'yes' because I had to be obedient and do as I was asked. This may sound bizarre, but that was how closed in my personality was. I was completely disassociated.

I can only remember always being like that. Even when bad stuff was happening to me, I still didn't experience the emotional pain associated with it; I somehow was cut off from it. When I found out that I wasn't adopted I did experience these bouts of suicidal thinking to 'finish it all, finish it all' and I did battle with that as if something inside me knew that it would be a bad thing to do. But even during the worst of the depression, I was somehow not aware of how deeply disassociated I was.

So, when Stuart asked me to marry him and I said 'yes', I didn't understand why he was so delighted. He decided that we would tell everyone about our engagement two weeks after the proposal, which was therefore a month after we'd met – this was partly because he was going on holiday and so he wanted to wait until he'd come back. I was very, very fearful of telling my parents, but I didn't know why I was afraid. However, during the actual event they didn't seem bothered at all. Mother asked Stuart lots of questions, like had he got a good job and was he going to be able to afford to look after me. But Father never said much. He just said, 'If that's what you want to do.'

So our engagement was generally accepted in my own home, but the thing that took us both by surprise was actually Stuart's parents; they weren't very happy. They'd heard the stories in the town about my family, so they tried to warn him off me – not in front of me, but when he was on his own. But Stuart remained adamant.

However, they embraced me into the family and actually became real parental figures to me and, in time, I learned to call them 'Mum and Dad'.

Chapter Seven: Repent and Be Baptised

Life went on and I continued to regularly read my Bible and therefore continued to learn more and more about God, as well as what the Bible says in its general outline. But everyday life wasn't any better and everything carried on as before. I struggled with this because it seemed from my reading of the Bible that walking with God should mean that you can be in a better place in life and that these bad things shouldn't happen. That's how I understood it at that time. But these bad things *were* still happening.

My emotional experience was just the same as before and my thinking about myself was the same; I still thought of myself as nobody and still told myself 'my name is *Nemo*'. The only thing that had changed was the feeling of God's presence being there and, from time to time on odd occasions, a heightened feeling of His presence. But I still got very, very depressed and I still battled constantly with that desire to end it all.

After I'd read the Bible for the first time, I then read it again. As I started to read things for a second time I would talk to Stuart and the people in the Bible study group and ask them, 'What does this passage mean?' or 'What does that mean?', assuming they would know. I found the passage referring to tithes and offerings in Malachi the Old Testament and I asked them about that. They explained that a 'tithe' meant a 'tenth' and that you were supposed to give a tenth of your income to God by giving it into the church collection plate, so I started doing that. (I don't look at it quite as rigidly as this nowadays!)

I also found a scripture in Acts where it reads, 'Repent and be baptised' (Acts 2:38). So, I asked Stuart what baptism meant and he told me all about the 'believer's baptism'. He used to go to a Baptist church, so he knew all about it. Being baptised was the first really difficult thing I had to do after becoming a Christian because I was afraid of water.

We used to have swimming lessons at school and the teacher who did the lessons believed in taking you to the deep end and pushing you in if you weren't learning well and keeping pace. Over time, there was me and a very overweight girl who both couldn't seem to keep pace, so both of us used to get pushed into the deep end of the pool. There actually came a point that we were both so frightened of the teacher and what might happen that we'd become physically sick with anxiety over it. Eventually we weren't allowed to go swimming anymore as the coach company kept charging the school to have the coach cleaned up! So for me, the thought of having to be baptised and go under the water was a big thing.

However, I knew that I had to be obedient to God, partly because I wanted to be, but if I'm honest, also partly because I had an overwhelming fear of God, which at that time wasn't the 'right' fear of God – the 'right' fear being a humble awe rather than fear of punishment.

It was because at that time I had no sense of the Fatherhood of God; it was an alien concept. So, I wanted to get baptised and obey because I was afraid of not doing as I was told (although there was also a part of me that did genuinely want to be obedient). About three months after I became a Christian, it was arranged for me to be baptised.

At this point in life, I had been in hospital quite a lot because of all the bladder problems and kidney infections that I had, which was probably down to a lot of the abuse. As timing would have it, I ended up needing to have a procedure done the week of my baptism. So, I was in hospital until the Friday before my baptism, which was on the following Sunday. It wasn't a major procedure, but it left me in a lot of pain for a few days.

On the Sunday, I was one of two people scheduled to be baptised; me and a young man (his baptism was the first I'd ever seen!). Nobody told me about how to go under the water without the water going up your nose and down your throat, so I just shut my eyes, held my breath and went under the water. Everything went up my nose and I just remember coming up and hanging onto the minister's robes for dear life, coughing and spluttering everywhere. I've never seen anyone else cause such a fuss when getting baptised; somebody even commented to me afterwards that I wasn't supposed to swallow half the pool!

However, what I also realised when I came up from the water was that all the ongoing pain from the medical procedure had totally gone. This was my first experience of God's healing power. All the pain had just gone as I came up out of the water and even though I didn't understand it all, I knew that God had done something. Nobody had mentioned or taught me that healing still happened today. Obviously, I had read about Jesus' miracles in the Bible but this was the first experience I'd ever had of God's healing touch in my life – in a small way, but in an instant way. I was therefore trying to process all this in my mind afterwards, but what made things confusing was that when I told people about it, although some people seemed really pleased, others just said, 'Well, those things don't happen today.' This was the beginning of regularly hearing those words: 'Those things don't happen today.' They were comments that began to disturb and unsettle me. They were words that were challenging to my new-found faith and I was to hear them a lot from then on.

Today we are living in a different time, when it's not so much 'those things don't happen today', rather more like, 'those things *don't matter as much today*'. I believe we are living in a post-charismatic, post-restoration, post-new church age whereby the place of reasonable argument and understanding has taken over. Of course our understanding matters, of course we want to study to be able to 'correctly [handle] the word of truth' (2 Timothy 2:15), but today we are in danger of losing the many aspects of the powerful working of the Spirit of God that were restored to the Church in the midst of the ushering in of the charismatic movement. Yesterday, today and forever, God is all-powerful, giving His children good gifts, to benefit the body (1 Corinthians 12), to build them up (1 Corinthians 14:12), to help them in building themselves up in their faith, to help us all to 'keep [ourselves] in God's love' (Jude 1:21) at a time of increasing intolerance to the Christian faith. We are not to be those who conform to this world and its ways of thinking (Romans 12:2); we are to look different because we are different. The Spirit is at work within us to change us 'from one degree of glory to another' (2 Corinthians 3:18, ESV) and that includes our using and moving in all the gifts He gives us, supernatural as well as natural.

Back then, in the minds of those around me, I was saying that the gift of healing existed for today, even though I didn't say that in as many words because I didn't understand it like that. Others around me were coming from the teaching that the gifts ceased with the coming of Jesus, the apostles, and the inauguration of the Church. And that was it, there were no more spiritual gifts after that, including the gift of healing. But at that time I didn't know or understand that cessationist argument. All I was saying was that something happened and it wasn't just because the pain had ceased, I had this feeling that the presence of God Himself; the Man in the Picture somehow enveloped me as I came up out of the pool, along with all the choking and sputtering!

Chapter Eight: Receiving the Gift of the Holy Spirit

Later in my Bible readings, when I came around to Acts 2 again and read 'Repent and be baptised', I knew I'd done that. But then it felt like I was reading the rest of the verse for the first time, which says, in the King James (Authorized) Version, 'and ye shall receive the gift of the Holy Ghost' – 'For the promise is unto you, and to your children, and to all that are afar off, even as many as the Lord our God shall call' (Acts 2:38-39). So, I started to think, 'What is the Holy Ghost?' and I embarked on searching the Scriptures for more. I wanted to know what the Holy Ghost was – or what we would now say, the 'Holy Spirit' – and I quickly began to see the Holy Spirit was mentioned everywhere and was referred to as a person rather than an 'it'. But nobody around me talked about the Holy Spirit.

As I continued to read, I began to see verses that spoke of being 'baptised with the Holy Spirit' (Acts 11:16), being 'filled with the Holy Spirit' (Acts 2:4), being 'carried along by the Holy Spirit' (2 Peter 1:21), the 'Holy Spirit comes on you' (Acts 1:8), the Holy Spirit bringing power and so on. I was so intrigued. What did it mean? I remember asking Stuart about what the baptism of the Holy Spirit was and it actually ended up being the beginning of a bit of a division between us both for a while. Up until that point I'd believed and taken everything that he'd been saying to me as the truth, but his response to my question had been, 'That's not for today' because he'd also been schooled in the line of thinking that all Holy Spirit-related activity stopped when the Church was inaugurated. 'We've got the Word, the Bible and that is our completeness, that's the perfect thing – so we don't need all that, it's not applicable for today.' I really battled with that way of thinking because by now I was reading 1 Corinthians again about the gifts of the Holy Spirit, for example prophecy and tongues, but particularly speaking in tongues (1 Corinthians 12,14).

At that point in time when I read the part about prophecy I never connected it to the scriptures in Jeremiah that I still so wanted to live by, because I still didn't understand what it was. But the gift of tongues, what was that? I asked Stuart about that too and he gave me what was now becoming the stock answer to nearly all of my questions, 'That's not for today.' And everyone else I asked said the same thing – everyone.

I found this extremely hard. Life at home was difficult and now this new Christian life was proving difficult too. But I had no idea of just how difficult things were going to get.

By this time I'd discovered some Christian bookshops and so I had started to read *Nine O'Clock in the Morning* and *The Holy Spirit and You* by Dennis and Rita Bennett and other books such as Kathyrn Kuhlman's *I Believe in Miracles*, or stories of a Yorkshire plumber called Smith Wigglesworth and other similar books. These books, like *Nine O'Olock in the Morning* but particularly *In the Day of Thy Power* plus '*Pray in the Spirit* written by Arthur Wallis (books now considered Christian classics), talked about the Spirit and speaking in tongues. As I read I was so filled with a deep, deep desire for the Holy Spirit to impact my life in the ways I was reading of; I was thirsty for this to happen in my life. Jesus said 'Let anyone who is thirsty come to me and drink' (John 7:37), which means we have to have a thirst for the things of God and only He can quench that thirst. Yet at the time, it felt as if I was doing something very wrong reading these books and I was careful to make sure I wasn't caught reading them!

So everyone around me was telling me that the Holy Spirit had finished His work well before the Bible came into existence and none of the gifts were for today. This set up a real crisis within me and I went through about six weeks of really struggling. I really didn't know what to think, how to choose to go forward, and there was also the whole Nemo battle: 'Everybody is telling me it's not for today, everybody else is right. I am wrong because I am nobody. So, am I trying to say that I am right and everyone else is wrong? That can't be true because I am nobody, I don't have an identity, I don't have any say in anything. I can't choose anyway.' It felt as if my whole being was being pulled apart.

At the end of about six weeks the crisis came to a head and I realised that this was causing me too many problems; I felt as though my whole inner being was being pulled to pieces trying to work it all out. I had read Acts 2 and both books of Corinthians and other instances in the Bible where the Holy Spirit is mentioned; for example, in the first book of Samuel, 'the Spirit of God came powerfully upon him' (1 Samuel 10:10; 11:6), and when Jesus was being 'led by the Spirit into the wilderness' (Matthew 4:1). Everywhere in the Bible I was reading about the Spirit! I thought, 'Well, if this isn't for today, then how can any of this book be for today? This is a dead book if these things don't happen today, so why am I going to church and trying to live by it? It must be wrong. How can some of it be for today and some of it not be for today?' That was my simplistic conclusion. So, I decided that I would pray for one last time, as if there was a God.

I decided I would ask God for this experience of being baptised in the Spirit and the experience of speaking in tongues and if it didn't happen and that 'presence' didn't come again, then it was all wrong and not for today and I was just allowing myself to get involved in some kind of cult or ritualistic way of life and so I would stop and never read the Bible again. That's the place I came to. I remember just getting down on my knees and naively thinking I could give God an ultimatum:

> OK, well I've read this part in Jeremiah and I believed that was You speaking to me, and when I got baptised I believed that was Your presence that I felt, but since then it's been one big mashing up of my brain because of what everyone has been telling me. So, can I have the Holy Spirit and speaking in tongues gift, and

> if it doesn't happen it must mean that everyone is right and it's not for today but, therefore, nothing can be for today, then, can it? So then I will just walk away from all this Christian stuff because clearly it won't be true.

What you might think then happened, didn't. I didn't have any sense or feeling of being baptised in the Holy Spirit, nor did I speak in tongues. But something did happen.

Whilst I was praying I had started to think again about the verse in Jeremiah, 'I appointed you as a prophet to the nations.' Out of all the verses that I'd previously read and felt God speak through, that was the one which had impacted me the most, yet I understood the least, because I didn't understand what a prophet was or looked like. In this prayer time kneeling down, this verse kept coming into my head with real focus and then the focus went to the last part of the sentence, 'a prophet to the nations.'

'Well, what is a prophet and what does it mean about the nations?' I found myself asking.

Then I began to be taken somewhere 'in my spirit', possibly even into a trance as in Peter's experience on the rooftop (Acts 10:9-16), though at the time I didn't call it that. I couldn't explain it or name it; for me it was a losing all sense of my surroundings – where I was, or what I had been praying about. It was like I was now seeing clearly and seeing something from God, hearing Him say things and having no doubt or question that this was God. Afterwards there was only worship and wonder in my heart. The questions had gone and I knew that these things were real and that I had a lifetime to come of living in expectancy for something and catching others up in that same expectancy. It was like a big picture opened up and caught me up within it.

I don't believe 'trances' happen very often, and I certainly don't believe that we should seek such experiences – we are only to seek

Him – but when they do happen there seems to be real significance in what occurs during that time. Acts 10 tells us that Peter 'fell into a trance' and then he had a vision of a sheet coming down in front of him full of 'unclean' animals. In this same trance Peter heard God telling him to kill and eat the animals and never to call anything 'impure' which God has made 'clean'. The end result of Peter listening to what God said to him during the trance was that the gospel began to go not just to the Jews but to the Gentiles also.

Whilst in the trance I began to have a series of visions about the nations and in particular the United Kingdom. I won't go into the detail of what they all were, except for one of those about the UK. I had a vision of the UK as if I were high, high up in the air looking down so that I could see the whole of the nation as if I were looking at a giant map. As I looked down, I could see little spots of light dotted all over the land and as I looked, they started getting brighter. As they got brighter, the ambient light around seemed to get darker and darker so that it was harder to see the outline of the UK. After a while the spots of light had become really clear and I then realised that they weren't just spots of light, they were fires, and the fires were like beacons burning brighter and brighter and brighter as if declaring a message. Everywhere across this UK 'map' I could see these fires, these beacons, and it was like the beacons were lighting up the UK. Then, all of a sudden, the fires almost instantaneously went across and up and down the map, all at the same time and became one huge fire engulfing the whole of the UK, and then the flames went licking across the seas towards other nations.

At the end of the vision whilst I was still in the trance, I heard a voice say, 'You will see this again in the natural as a confirming sign of this which you have seen in the spiritual. This is from Me, and you will then see the same sign again when these things are imminent.'

And that was the end of the encounter.

I then came out of the trance and realised that I was still on the floor, kneeling down in my front room. I'd been into His presence without realising it. But now, afterwards, it was like the aftermath of that presence was in the room. You know, when somebody with a heavy perfume has been in a room and then they've gone, but the perfume is still there and so the presence of the person is still around even though they've left? It was like that. The aftermath of that presence was still around me in the room. Then I wrote everything down.

So on that day I never walked away from my new-found faith because of all the 'this is not for today' comments. Because I knew now that all these things *were* for today because this experience was so vivid and God's presence so very real. Even though my prayer wasn't answered in the way that I thought it would be and I still didn't speak in tongues, I did have a life-changing encounter with God. And I also knew that it all had something to do with the Jeremiah passage, 'I appointed you as a prophet to the nations.'

Looking back, I see myself as being like this block of butter in the fridge that was rock-hard and that these experiences caused a slight softening in me before something began to start to really have an effect on me.

It was actually not very long after this encounter that I experienced what I would describe as being baptised in the Spirit. I was still in a place of being really desirous of receiving these things but from that encounter onwards, I didn't dare ask anymore. But a week or two later, we were at one of Stuart's friends' house with several other people. One of them, a man who I hadn't met before, clearly had had this experience of the baptism in the Spirit and speaking in tongues.

Everyone in the room, therefore, was engaged in a big discussion about it all and everyone (except the man and his friend) in the room was saying, 'It's not for today.' This particular man then turned to me and said, 'What do you think?' Well, I'd never been asked for my opinion before and had never given one, so I didn't know how to handle that at all. Stuart had just been asked what he thought and he had said, 'No, it's not for today. We have the Bible now, we don't need that, the perfect is here.' And so when the man then turned and asked me, I just repeated what Stuart had said verbatim, 'It's not for today, we have the Bible now…' and so the discussion carried on.

But somewhere inside I knew it *was* for today and I felt so frustrated that these things were being said, yet I couldn't find the way into this 'life in the Spirit'. I so desperately wanted it all to happen to me.

Before we went home we normally had a little prayer time in order to pray for one another, just a five-minute thing. So, we had this prayer time and the five-minute thing went on a bit. The man who had provoked discussion earlier and could speak in tongues was doing so quietly and the other person who had come with him was also quietly murmuring in tongues. I thought to myself, 'How can they do that?'

After a few minutes, the man who had asked for my opinion stood up and came to me and said, 'You want to be baptised in the Spirit, don't you?' And I just said, 'Yes.' He never said anything of what he was going to do but I knew something was going to happen and I felt very apprehensive. He was standing up at the time and I was sitting down holding Stuart's hand because I was really frightened. This man put his hand on my head and just said, in really old-fashioned King James version kind of language, 'Receive ye the Holy Ghost.' And I felt like I'd been hit by a lightning bolt that went right through my body.

You know in those cartoons when they've just been electrocuted by something and the character is depicted as shaking and having their hair standing on end? Well, I felt like that. It was like electricity was flowing right through me and coming out of my fingertips. Stuart yelped and let go of my hand immediately! He told me afterwards that he felt like he'd been burnt. I then fell on my knees and started spilling out these words, speaking in tongues at the top of my voice; not just two or three words over and over, but a full-blown set of languages in different kinds of tongues, all at the top of my voice. I was speaking more fluently in unknown languages than I ever could speak in English!

And I knew that I knew that the presence that from time to time had come to me, was well and truly in me. The Man in the Picture was here and I had access to Him at all times. I don't know how I knew that. But I knew.

Chapter Nine:
Outside the Fold

The rest of the people in the room who had been saying, 'This does not happen today' were disturbed and perplexed by what was happening to me in front of them. They knew me as quiet and hardly able to string a sentence together, so this was worrying for them. It affected Stuart too and messed with his theology, but the others thought, 'Wow, we've got into demonic stuff here!' So now the people around me had shifted from thinking, 'This doesn't happen today' to 'This is the work of demons'. Although Stuart didn't think like that, he was battling and trying to process it all because this was now outside his experience and understanding. I knew that it was not demonic because I knew that it was the same God that had come to me before and that had caused me to throw all of those tablets away and find Him, and that this same God had kept me alive and shown me something of what was to happen in the world and the UK particularly. I never questioned or thought that this experience was not from God.

The man who had prayed for me told me that I should testify and tell people at church what had happened. So, I went back to my local church and the following Sunday asked whether I could tell people of something that had happened to me. They agreed and said they were happy for me to do that, but when I stood up and told them, it was not received at all well. That was the moment which began what turned out to be quite an intense and lengthy period of real difficulty, even persecution, because in their eyes this was the work of demons; what had happened to me was demonic and I was now possessed of demons.

It was around that time that I began to realise that not everyone in that church was even a Christian! I had just assumed that because they were there every week, sitting in the pews, they were Christians, but actually I began to discover that there were quite a number of people who were merely what I thought of as 'religious'; in those days, if you went to church it was seen as a good thing to do in the community. So, after testifying about what had happened to me, people seemed to be on a mission to 'work on me' to try to get me exorcised from the demons and respectably quiet again. They wanted to get me back to being the *Nemo* that inside I still felt that I was and everyone around me appeared to prefer me to be.

However, two or three people who had experienced the same thing but hadn't told anyone began to own up that this had also happened to them. Together we were just hungry; we wanted to seek God more and we wanted more of whatever this was.

At this point, Stuart and I were now married. From the day that we met he knew that I was to be his wife, so we were married the following May. We'd planned a long engagement, originally about eighteen months, because obviously we didn't really know each other. But our plans changed.

Stuart was coming to my house on a particular day to meet me, but at that time there was also a big argument going on in the house. The end result was Father hit me with his fist which sent me flying across the room. I then ran out of the house with my nose bleeding just as Stuart was coming up the garden path.

'What's the matter?' Stuart asked.

'Father just hit me,' I replied.

'Right, we're getting married,' Stuart said. So, all our plans were brought forward and we married in May 1973.

Once married we moved into a little house of our own that we'd managed to get a mortgage for – Stuart used the proceeds from the sale of his motorbike for a deposit. We were the only married couple in the little group that was wanting to press into the things of the Spirit and the only ones with our own home, so we started hosting a meeting every week, like a Bible study, to look at everything about the Spirit in more detail.

However, most of the church, including the minister, didn't like what we were doing and eventually it resulted in some wild stories going around. Apparently, I was corrupting people. I had corrupted Stuart, because by now Stuart had been baptised in the Spirit and spoke in tongues, and now one or two others had also received the gift of speaking in tongues whilst praying in our living room. Those were blessed times, but those same times led to me being seen as a perpetrator of evil; someone who was leading people into a cult that was demonic.

Unfortunately, around that time, two things happened which increased the pressure and brought everything to a head for my local church. The first was the release of a horror film called *The Exorcist*, a box office hit which everyone was talking about. The second incident was the sad case of a man in a nearby village who had sought help from his local vicar, been referred for 'exorcism' but then immediately afterwards had gone home and brutally murdered his wife and even the family dog.

These two things were both widely reported upon nationally, and the fears and imaginings of the people around me were fuelled even more. All manner of things were being said to be taking place in our home when our few friends visited.

As a result, I was labelled as a 'witch'. Apparently, I was 'a witch from a long line of witches' – that's what was said about me. To a lot of people my eccentric mother looked and behaved like one, so I suppose it's not surprising that this was said. The unhappy minister of my local church therefore said that he wanted to see me, and I was summoned. When I met him in the vestry of the church building he ended up completely losing his temper with me. He was adamant that it was the devil that was at work in me.

'I want to help you, I want to exorcise the demons!' he said.

'But it's not! I know it's God,' I protested.

Then he just lost it and shouted, 'The very devil himself is using you!'

In the Methodist denomination, the ministers moved around from time to time and we knew that this particular minister was moving on in the few weeks following that episode. Unfortunately ,however, he'd prepared the new minister as to what to expect from us, so as soon as he arrived he asked to see us both in the manse – a house belonging to the church that the minister lived in.

He made himself very clear from the start and informed us that he'd heard about everything. When I tried to convince him by saying 'Actually, it's not like that, it's God,' he replied, 'Well, I'm not having that in my church!'

He continued, 'Either you stop or you leave the church. You can make a pact with me now that you will not speak in tongues or prophesy, you will not refer to speaking in tongues or to prophecy, you will not speak to anyone about speaking in tongues and prophecy and you will stop talking about all this stuff to do with the Spirit, because that is not going to be in my church. Or you must leave.'

Stuart and I just looked at each other and said, 'Well, we'll have to leave, then.'

The minister then replied, 'Well, let me tell you, there is no church in this town where you can go and do these things. I'll give you some time to think about it and you can let me know before the weekend.'

So, at some point before Sunday, we wrote a letter that said that we couldn't just stop doing all of those things because for us that was part of what we believed God was doing and therefore, bearing in mind what he'd said, unfortunately we'd have to leave the church. We put the letter through the letter box. And we were never welcome in that church again.

This was actually very sad for me because it was the place in which I'd come to the Christian faith and it was where we'd been married. We also then quickly found out what he'd meant at the end of his talk; he'd spoken to every church leader in town about us. We therefore weren't welcome in the Anglican church, the United Reformed

Church, the Salvation Army or the Catholic church. Along with the Methodist church, those were all of the churches that were around in the town at that time. We simply weren't welcome at any of them nor allowed in for any reason.

By this time, the stories about what I was supposedly getting up to were rife and becoming increasingly fantastical. Apparently, I was sacrificing cats and using their blood to daub around other people's property, performing 'exorcisms' (as in the film) on unsuspecting people, casting spells and putting curses on people I didn't like by speaking them onto a cassette tape and then winding the tape around people's property. All manner of things were spreading like wildfire around the neighbourhood to the point where local people wouldn't even speak to me or acknowledge me. If I was walking down the street and someone was coming towards me, they would cross the road and walk on the other side. People at work were also no longer speaking to me. The lies and ostracising had now gone way beyond the churches and Christian circles.

Eventually, the whole town avoided me because of the rumours. If I went into the bank, the person behind the counter would not interact with me, so Stuart would have to go to the bank instead. If I went into a shop, the shopkeeper would not serve me, so Stuart would have to help with and pay for the shopping. The only person who carried on talking to me, when necessary, was my GP, and I felt that he had made his mind up about me from the start and couldn't be bothered about me. I believed that he had decided, given my history, that I was 'mentally subnormal' and would never be anything other than permanently depressed and therefore permanently in need of drugs. So, all he would do was look up and say, 'Oh, it's you,' and write a prescription for more tranquillisers and more antidepressants. That's how he managed me.

My life became one long round of trying to cope with virtual isolation, with only Stuart and a couple of others in our little group standing with me. The one saving grace was that by this time I worked out of town, in the city of Sheffield, where no one knew about any of this.

Our little group still continued. We would just pray by ourselves on Sunday mornings and read our Bible together, and then on Friday nights we would have this little meeting together where three or four brave souls, who still believed in everything to do with the Holy Spirit, would join us. But it did literally decrease down to about five of us and eventually on Sundays just the two of us, because the others either went where God was leading them, or just couldn't cope with the reactions they had by being associated with us. I was 'the witch', the ringleader who had led everyone astray.

Even Father, who hardly ever spoke to me, said, 'What are you up to? What are you doing?' because of all the things he'd heard from his workmates. I think it embarrassed him. I would try to reassure him, but he'd just say, 'Well, I've heard some right rumours and I don't like them!' I would reply, 'Well, they're not true,' but it didn't seem to matter; he seemed more concerned with how it made him look.

So I had to cope with even my non-Christian, non-churchgoing family querying what I was supposedly 'up to', and the fact that everywhere I went I couldn't get anyone to interact with me. It was like I was isolated from a whole community. But then I already had in my thinking the idea that I was meant to be isolated: 'Well, I'm *Nemo* anyway, I'm invisible, I don't exist.' So, everything that was happening to me was just reinforcing that way of thinking. *Nemo* was really in full force and I just went into an existence of coping the best way I could and getting Stuart to interact with others on my behalf. I didn't have a voice of my own; except on my own in prayer times with God.

Chapter Ten: The Clamour of Many Voices

During those times, and on other occasions since then, to be able to pray in tongues for a length of time did so much to sustain me. When words failed in prayer and faith was tested, it was as if praying in tongues gave just the right words to God, pouring out the difficulties of the battle and the struggle to forgive, to turn the other cheek and ignore the comments. I'd speak in tongues, on and on, sometimes for hours, until eventually something supernaturally poured back in of the greatness of God, His sovereignty, His rule and ability to go before me, vindicate, carry, strengthen and keep my feet firmly in place on the path of faith in Him. Then finally I would return to that place of eternal perspective that comes from being hidden in Him: 'For you died, and your life is now hidden with Christ in God' (Colossians 3:3).

But the suicidal depression aspect was still there and was still really, really bad; it was trying to take over. It would rise up in me and grow in me until it was so big that I didn't know what to do. So, even though I hadn't carried through my plan the night I'd become a Christian, I was still struggling all the time not to go ahead with it. I knew from reading the text in Jeremiah 1:5, 'before you were born I consecrated you … I knew you' (ESV) that it was wrong. It was wrong because He has made us holy, is making us holy and He has paid a great price for us. I knew before God that it was a wrong thing to do but I still didn't know how to not think about it and how to keep it at bay – the urge was so bad.

Negative and difficult thoughts would fill my head like a constant stream. Thoughts about all the things people were saying; I would be hearing mother's voice over and over: 'You're mental, you, you need a doctor', 'You're nobody. Who do you think you are?', 'You're worthless. Nobody wants you around.' Or I'd be listening in my head to my father's voice: 'You're useless', 'You're a clumsy idiot', 'You're stupid and good for nothing.' I would have the taunts of the school bullies or the faithless words of the teachers joining in with the clamour of the many things my brain had recorded from home over the years that made up my life to that point. And these thoughts ruled my life; I even called myself stupid and useless, reinforcing the thoughts daily. They dictated to me the same story of worthlessness and repeatedly suggested to me that there was only one way out, only one way to shut down all these voices, to take my own life. All this was constantly going on in my own head.

Because the doctor gave me prescriptions for all manner of things – antidepressants, tranquillisers, Valium, I always had access to lots of tablets. So, I would always have a great stash of them with me wherever I went, either in my handbag or in my coat pockets. And I was ready at all times to swallow them and end it all.

Nobody outside our home was aware of this overwhelming desire to kill myself. It never occurred to me to talk about it to anyone, though I'd constantly be telling Stuart: 'I might as well kill myself,' or 'I don't want to be here, I'm not meant to be here, 'I'm not meant to exist.' By now I often wondered if he was regretting having married me.

Outside of our home I'd meet people with Stuart or we occasionally went to find fellowship with groups in other towns who did believe that the spiritual gifts were for today. When we went to join with them, I used to enjoy the meetings – how wonderful it was to be there, lapping up the sense of the presence of God in the meetings. We might have lunch or coffee with people and Stuart would do all the talking. But I was still this shut off, disassociated and suicidal person.

In some of those meetings, I'd now got to a point where I'd realised that if you spoke in an unknown language, there should then follow an interpretation. The Bible says, 'the one who speaks in a tongue should pray that they may interpret what they say' (1 Corinthians 14:13). So, I said to God, 'I don't just want to speak in tongues, your word says I have to interpret.' My thinking was still, 'I have to, because He said it.' So, I prayed to be able to interpret, and then had actually begun to do that in the meetings that we went to. It's strange – I could do that but I still couldn't string a sentence together in normal conversation in that same environment! And I was still battling with the suicidal feelings.

Frequently, a tongue would come and I would interpret it. In those circumstances I would feel like God was saying, 'This is what that means…' and I'd just repeat what I felt I was hearing. However, what I'd originally felt God had spoken to me about in terms of prophecy was becoming more apparent because from time to time something would happen whereby I felt as if God was saying to me, 'I want you to say this…' and I would speak in the first person as if God had said it. It was generally mostly based on Scripture and because I was mainly swamped in the Authorized Version, most of what came out of my mouth was 'yea' and 'thee' and 'thou' – old-fashioned language. So, I suppose that was the beginning of me starting to prophesy, but I still hadn't associated that with prophecy.

At first I would hear God seemingly from nowhere but then I began to find things would come from a place where I would just know that people in the meeting were feeling low or 'under something'. Then I shifted from God saying to me, 'Tell them this…' almost from a void, to knowing that these people needed something and so I'd say, 'God, these people need something.' Then He'd say, 'Tell them this…' and so I began to understand the concept of bringing that which comes in order to comfort, build up and strengthen people (1 Corinthians 14:3) without realising that was what I was doing.

But a battle was still raging wildly every day; I needed that same comfort and strength so I needed to be continually filled with the Spirit. In my everyday walk with God I was speaking in tongues and doing it a lot because I'd learned that speaking in tongues kept me going, it edified me, built me up, strengthened me, and I was 'sensing things in the Spirit' when I did it. I was also prophesying, although I didn't yet know that's what it was. All that was happening, but at the same time the suicidal thoughts were still tormenting me and waging war with my mind.

Behind closed doors I was trying in my relationship with Stuart to keep doing what I thought he wanted me to do, to be the obedient wife. Stuart had never given me any set of expectations or indicated in any way that I wasn't living up to his idea of a good wife, though of course by now I'd read Proverbs 31 many times and I knew I didn't measure up to what a good wife should be like.

I had never questioned a word Stuart ever said to me apart from the issue about baptism in the Spirit. For example, if we were planning a holiday, Stuart would say, 'This is where we're going on holiday.' I'd agree, 'Yes.' He'd say, 'I've looked at some places to stay and I've picked this one out.' 'OK,' I'd reply. That's how I'd converse with him because I couldn't choose. There wasn't very much else to the conversation!

Stuart always very much kept me under his wing and looked after me, especially during the years where he knew the whole town was ostracising me. But I still wasn't my own person. It wasn't Stuart's fault, but the disassociation stood in the way. What would happen was that the stress of it all would build and build and build up in me to the point that I just wouldn't know how to handle it. Then, as we were having one of these supposed 'talks' about a holiday, for example – where it was actually him doing all the talking and me just saying 'yes' – all of a sudden something would blow inside of me. And I would erupt into a terrible rage that I was unable to contain.

If there were holiday brochures on the table, I'd tear them into shreds and throw them at him. Stuart would say in despair, 'What's the matter? What's the matter?' And then I'd get cross with him because he didn't know what the matter was. But I didn't even know what the matter was myself. So, I'd try to hit him and he would try to hold me and I'd be pummelling with my fists on his chest and would pull his hair until it came out by the roots, desperately lashing out in a rage that I had no control over.

Somewhere deep inside I wondered what on earth was happening to me, and why. I knew that I needed to stop, but I couldn't, it was like something had taken hold of me. For the first time in my life I was beginning to experience something other than fear – raging anger.

Previously, I'd had no sense or feelings of anger, but now it was an emotion that would randomly come exploding out of me and I had no control over it. I didn't 'feel' it in a 'that's made me angry' kind of way, it was as if every now and again a great volcano would erupt inside of me and then I would physically lash out and hurt Stuart and sometimes myself in the process. I could not control myself when this happened.

Inside, I was saying, 'What am I doing? Why is this happening to me?' I didn't want it to be like that. I never seemed to see any signals that the rage was building up, and I didn't know where it was coming from, but when it did erupt, it was as if until I'd got to a certain point where I'd worn myself out, I just couldn't stop it. Then afterwards I would be extremely remorseful and feel even worse about myself. Without realising it, I was repeating the pattern of my father.

Fortunately, I never significantly physically hurt Stuart because he's a strong man and I was a little stick back then. The thing that probably physically hurt him the most was when I pulled his hair. However, emotionally I was tearing him apart. He didn't know how to help me, how to make life better for me, or what on earth was going on. No, physically the damage wasn't that much, but in every other way it was torment for him whilst I would be totally out of control.

If there was a mug of coffee on the table I would pick it up and throw it. I remember mugs smashing and coffee running down the walls.

Then Stuart would try to hold me until I was totally exhausted. But then I would become morose, so morose that I couldn't speak at all because I didn't want to be like that and didn't understand why I was like it. And then the whole *Nemo* battle would arise in full force: 'You cause damage, you hurt people, you should not be here, you don't exist, make it so that you don't exist. Take the tablets, take the tablets.'

What I didn't realise at the time was that this was the voice of an enemy; no longer was I listening to the voice of my human tormentors, now I was listening to the voice of the enemy who comes to rob and to steal. I was bound up by lies that were so familiar to me that they seemed to be truths. I was constantly rehearsing them in my head, constantly giving myself over to lies and therefore constantly walking back into darkness.

And so as soon as Stuart let go of me I would rush out of the door and set off running, and then I would walk and walk and walk. It didn't matter what the weather was like; I would walk through any weather. I've been out in the lashing rain, the hot sun, snow and wind. I've been known to walk around thirty miles in that state. And inside, all the time, I would be listening to this voice, 'Take the pills, you don't exist, you are *Nemo*, you don't exist, you are nothing, nobody, take the pills.' The pills would be in my pockets where I always kept them and my hand would play with them, turning them over and over as I walked. I would then just keep walking and walking until I was utterly exhausted.

At the point where I became so physically exhausted that my brain finally shut down its taunts, it would be as if 'this time I've got through again'. I'd got through another round until next time; something had quieted and left me. My thoughts had evaporated in the face of exhaustion and all the taunting voices of darkness had left me.

Then I would have to try to find out how to get home. Sometimes I didn't know where I was so I'd have to keep walking until I found a telephone box – there were no mobile phones then.

Stuart would be really, really worried, wondering where I was, and so he'd drive around, often in a borrowed car, trying to find me. When he eventually tracked me down, he'd take me home and then I'd go to bed to sleep it off. I'd sleep for two, three or even four days, just completely 'out of it' and catatonic. If I was supposed to be going to work then I'd have to take sick leave or holiday because I'd just be unable to function.

It was like a living hell for both of us.

Chapter Eleven: The Nature of Control

What I realise now, but didn't understand then, was that evil speaks and entices us. I was listening to an evil spirit speaking to me. It spoke to me in a similar way to that which God spoke to me, though I knew it wasn't God's voice; it was different, it was dark and God was light. I knew it was a 'bad thing.' I started to feel like the classic Jekyll and Hyde case. I'd read the book by Robert Louis Stephenson, and by then I'd seen the film and it was a horribly good comparison with how I was. Later on a TV show called *The Incredible Hulk* came out which tells the story of a man who has been infected by something and all of a sudden he would burst into anger. He'd then turn green and change into a monster twice as big, and cause massive amounts of damage and destruction. It was like that. I was like that. What was wrong with me?

The problem was that I believed the lies. I believed what my mother said, 'You're mental, you, you need a doctor.' I believed I was mentally ill and that I needed a doctor. I believed my mother was right. I also believed I was 'a witch from a long line of witches'. I believed the lies, every lie. What I was feeling and what I was listening to had become the truth to me. Everything bad, I believed. But the biggest thing of all that I believed was that I was *Nemo*; nobody. I believed that this false non-identity was my real identity. '*Nemo* is your existence. *Nemo* is no-man. *Nemo* is invisible.' And it was *Nemo*, or rather the tormenting suicidal spirit, that spoke to me and said, 'You are *Nemo.*'

Nemo had invaded my whole personality and that's what I was chained into as effectively as the demon-possessed man of Gadarene had been chained (Luke 8:27). *Nemo* was what I had christened myself and *Nemo* was what I had become: nothing, no identity, nobody, destined to stay in the background, unseen and unheard.

The enemy tries to do this to the Church – believers in Christ – as well, to convince us about a false identity, to rob us of our worth and value and make us think that we are nothing, nobody, with no identity, that we shouldn't get in the way or be heard, consequently robbing us of our voice. But the Church has been set free and can rise up and find her voice!

This is a time to expect the intervention of God into our ordinary lives. It is through the lives of ordinary men and women like you and I that the extraordinary power of God can be displayed. It is a time for us to speak out, to be at ease with who we are as the children of God, those who have been redeemed, 'bought at a price' (1 Corinthians 6:20), set free from the power of the enemy and have the Holy Spirit within us. We are those who, contrary to what the world and the enemy would say, *do* have a voice. The world needs to hear the voice of the Church. You were set free to speak, you are not *Nemo*, you are a child of God, you are not mute, you do have a voice. The Church *does* have a voice and *is* meant to be heard.

In the book of 1 Kings we are introduced to King Ahab's wife, Jezebel (1 Kings 16:31). She was a mistress of devious control and manipulation in order to gain what she wanted.

Jezebel sought to kill the prophets; those who spoke out for God. Even Elijah, God's great prophet, became afraid of her and hid himself away, sinking into the depths of despair and suicidal thinking (see 1 Kings 18 and 19). Even though he had seen and been a part of powerful acts of God he was robbed of his voice by his fear of this woman. Here are some the characteristics of Jezebel which we can read about in 1 and 2 Kings, and Revelation 2:

she wanted to destroy the work of God
she controlled and manipulated to achieve what she wanted
she worshipped false gods
she used her sexuality to allure and be immoral
she brought about despair and death
she incited fear

she attempted to destroy the prophets
she threatened those who got in her way
she deceived and was deceiving
she assumed an authority she didn't actually have
she incited accusation and division
she attempted to isolate people
she robbed others of what was rightfully theirs (such as Naboth's vineyard, see 1 Kings 21)

In my family home, this is what Mother was like. She would deceive people and manipulate events to go her way; in particular she would manipulate in her relationship with Father, who in turn went along with whatever she suggested. When Father was reaching a boiling point of frustration, Mother would somehow always convince him that I was 'to blame' and the beatings would eventually come.

I learned to recognise these characteristics long before I read of Jezebel in the Bible. I learned to see it as it was happening, seeing something taking over in front of my eyes that was going to try to kill me. That's what it felt like at the time, but what I was unknowingly encountering was the power of an evil spirit operating in the same way and with the same characteristics as Jezebel in the Bible. Gradually as I grew up, I became so acutely aware of this being the big thing to avoid that I lived in a constant state of tension, waiting for its next appearance, and I looked for ways to try to stop it. I would try to make sure all the chores were done and the house was tidy so that Mother would not begin her manipulative tactics to effect yet another beating from Father.

But there are also things that affect you inside, in your thinking and emotions when you are subjected to this kind of controlling behaviour. As we read about Jezebel, we see how what she did affected those around her, and we can see then how an evil spirit can work in the same way, causing us to feel or believe things about ourselves even to the point of making us ill. Although I need to add –the things listed below may not always be the result of a spirit. Of course, all these things can occur because of other things which are happening to us in life, perhaps as a result of our current circumstances, such as losing a job, or an extended time of illness. The important thing is to be able to recognise what's going on by revelation from the Holy Spirit rather than see this as a set of equations which add up in our minds. Today we really do need to pray for the spiritual gift of 'distinguishing between spirits' (1 Corinthians 12:10) and not make quick assumptions.

However, here are some of the things we can end up feeling or encountering when this evil spirit is or has been at work:

I am failing or I am a failure;
Things are not working out as they should;
I have no choices and no valid opinion;
Feeling inclined to give up and retreat to worldly things or ways of thinking;
Having thoughts of sexual immorality or a constant fear of that happening;
Feeling ill, bouts of sickness, even causing me to have thoughts about death, dying, or taking my own life;
Being fearful (of whatever);
Holding back from moving out in gifts or witness, constantly contesting my faith;
Having feelings of being 'conned', 'used', or 'tricked';
Questioning my own authority, or causing my authority to be belittled or overturned;
Feeling isolated, and/or isolating myself;
Feeling lonely and/or tempted to withdraw;
Feeling robbed – this can lead to being robbed of vision, of strength and of my voice.

Any of these things can happen when this spirit is at work, either in a psychological sense or in a physical sense, metaphorically or actually. I was muted by this spirit in a real, physical way through what it was doing in my inner being, causing me to see myself as having no voice. I was terrified of it, anxious all the time that it might arise and come after me. I felt powerless, lonely, weak and belittled. Most of all, it robbed me of my own confidence in myself, of any sense of being able to choose, to have an opinion, to make any sound judgement, or even to speak.

In time, being under the effects of these things can cause our behaviour to adapt to it accordingly and so, much of my behaviour became shaped by living under the influence of this controlling and manipulative spirit.

I withdrew even more, became even more disassociated and resolved never to step out of line, never trust anyone or anything, never be seen or heard… 'I am *Nemo*, I do not exist. But on the other hand, now I belong to God. I should trust God. To prophesy means to have to step out and speak. I have to allow myself to be heard, to be seen.' A war of unresolvable conflicts had begun to rage within me.

In summary, the enemy uses these manipulative, controlling tactics to rob us of our inheritance in God as surely as Jezebel robbed Naboth of his family vineyard (1 Kings 21). It is worth reading that account, if you have the time.

Chapter Twelve: Build Yourself Up in Faith

When a person becomes a Christian, and particularly after baptism in the Spirit, often their problems can seem to get worse. This is not a negative, it is a sign that the reality of what has happened in their spirit, the life and light at the core of who they are, is beginning to challenge the darkness in the rest of their life. For me, I think what was happening at that time was that having been baptised in the Spirit, the Spirit of God was challenging *Nemo* within me and that's why it felt like Jekyll and Hyde were going head to head.

I could be in a Christian meeting where there was wonderful praise and worship and I would be immersed in worshipping God and so aware of my sin, even though I hadn't got a clue why I was like I was. But then at the same time, I would know that God was telling me to say something specific, because people needed to be strengthened and encouraged. So, I would say it and people would be strengthened in their walk with God, yet I would continue to remain shut in to this battle with *Nemo*: 'You are Nemo. Take the tablets.' I couldn't see that at the time I was just tolerating and giving way to all the lies that I was so firmly bound up in by the enemy, through ignorance and blindness.

But we are not meant to tolerate these things; we can be bound up, as I was, through having been caught up in difficult situations; we can even fall into behaving like this with others if we don't realise what the enemy is doing, but we are meant to reject the lies that have bound us. We must not tolerate the enemy's work within us but recognise it as spiritual attack and resist the enemy. Hebrews 10:39 says 'we do not belong to those who shrink back...' We are not to allow these things to cause us to retreat, rather we press on in faith.

As we read about Jezebel in the Bible, seeing how the enemy works like that today, we read in 2 Kings 9:30-37 that it was those who had been most weakened by Jezebel who served her and were used by her; those were the people who finally dealt with her by pushing her out of an upper window. When we have been tolerating and listening to the lies of the enemy, being brought low by these things, we need to recognise that it is an enemy at work; it is a spiritual attack and we who have been affected are the ones who have to turn away from the lies. We need to declare that we are no longer going to tolerate them in our lives and 'push them out of the window', as it were, by saying, 'I will have no more.' We therefore no longer allow our thinking, our actions and reactions, to be led by lies and we get back into the truth of what God has called us to be and do.

Allowing ourselves to develop patterns of thinking based on lies means we are giving ourselves to something that is in opposition to the truth; we are rejecting the truth in favour of the lie. In John 8:32 Jesus says, 'you will know the truth, and the truth will set you free', but if we reject the truth then the truth cannot help us. To be set free by the truth means we need to embrace it and turn away from the lie.

However, before I realised this, I couldn't see any pattern for when *Nemo* seemed to wage war more strongly. I couldn't see any cause for the times when I would just explode; it all just felt random to me because in the interim I just got on with life, relieved that the battle had abated somewhat for a while.

In private I spoke in tongues a lot of the time because I knew that it somehow helped me.

The Bible tells us in 1 Corinthians 12 of gifts which are given by the Holy Spirit, one of these being 'speaking in different kinds of tongues' (v. 10). We can then read on and discover that another of the gifts is that of 'interpretation of tongues' and Paul then goes on to teach in chapter 14 about the importance of using these gifts correctly in the church, only speaking out a message in tongues when we know there is someone present who can interpret. But for me there is also enough evidence in the Bible to understand that the gift of tongues is something I can use every day in my own prayer life. I don't need an interpreter when I'm on my own with God, when I'm wanting to relate to Him, to communicate with Him, to know His presence with me.

So, as well as praying in my own English language, I just poured out my heart to Him in 'tongues'.

Paul writes in 1 Corinthians 14:18, 'I thank God that I speak in tongues more than all of you' – where did Paul do that if not on his own in his personal prayers to God? Romans 8:26-27 tells us: 'We do not know what we ought to pray for, but the Spirit himself intercedes for us through wordless groans. And he who searches our hearts knows the mind of the Spirit, because the Spirit intercedes for God's people in accordance with the will of God.' Do these verses refer to speaking in tongues? Some think so, but I think they are speaking about a work of the Spirit in us that is far bigger and wider than just speaking in an unknown tongue. What this does say to me is that I am weak, that I need the Spirit to help me to know what to pray, that my prayers go beyond just the words that I might choose to use, that the Spirit knows my innermost being and its 'groans' in a way which I do not, and that He is interceding for me.

When I speak in tongues in my prayer times, I am acknowledging my weakness before God. My inability to know what to pray gives way to praying as the Spirit gives me the words, and it means I am communicating all that I need to communicate in this moment. Paul tells us in 1 Corinthians 14:2,4 that the person who speaks in an unknown tongue 'does not speak to people but to God' and 'Anyone who speaks in a tongue edifies themselves, but the one who prophesies edifies the church.' So, when I use tongues in my prayers I am 'edifying', or 'building myself up', in my faith; I am choosing to trust Him in my weakness and I am getting even more in touch with His strength for me in that weakness (2 Corinthians 12:9).

There were dark days, difficult circumstances and situations where I felt overwhelmed by the battle, days when the blackness of depression settled on me and the urge to 'opt out' of life came again. In determining to try to pray in those times, I began to speak in tongues and found myself doing so for hours, sometimes into most of the night, knowing I was praising Him, knowing I was lifting my spirit to Him, knowing that whatever was wrong inside was being carried to Him, and knowing that somehow praying like this was lifting me slowly out of a mire of negative thoughts and deep darkness.

In those times, as I prayed in tongues I found I began to slip into my own language, asking Him to move because He was in control, He was sovereign, He could do all things. And then I began to start extolling the greatness of God and eventually the presence of God came, something lifted and my perspective changed, and I would be able to get through another day.

I find today that so many Christians who can speak in tongues actually don't do it in their private prayer times that much anymore. I couldn't have said back then why it helped me so much to speak in tongues, but I knew that it did help. It is such a powerful 'weapon' in our armoury, to help us build ourselves up in our 'most holy faith' and keep ourselves in the love of God (Jude 20-21). Today, as I have mentioned earlier, I keep hearing that the prevailing thinking is, 'These things don't really matter that much today.' All of the supernatural gifts of God are wonderful gifts, given to us by the Holy Spirit to help us in our daily walk with Him, in our being able to fight the fight of faith and in our being able to proclaim the gospel, the good news, to others. 'These things' *do* matter and are as living, necessary and crucial for us today as they ever were. Let's be zealous to see them in operation in our corporate life together and in our own private times with the Father.

Despite experiencing times of having sensed the nearness of God, the eruptions of anger did keep randomly happening. I felt tormented and totally out of control of my own feelings and behaviour, and it led me to despair.

As I read the Bible more and more, I began to realise that God is three in one and so I had read about God as the Father. Through everything I read about God as the Father I had absolutely no sense of encountering Him in that way.

I knew about God as the Son and understood what He went through on the cross. I understood that in its theological sense, though I had no feeling of what that must have been like. God the Son was still like that picture in my little book, for me He was the Man in the Picture. And then to me at that time, God the Holy Spirit was like an ethereal power, or 'blanket of strength' that came upon me and was in me and enabled me to keep going and to say things from time to time. I'd been reading about a relationship of peace and grace, and a God who cared for me, yet I couldn't seem to know Him as 'Father', or as someone who was kind and merciful. I was afraid all the time; afraid that God, who was infinitely stronger and more powerful than my earthly father ever was, was also poised to punish me for the slightest misdemeanor.

All that I read about the Father God was so totally outside of my experience that I became even more confused. There was then another war set up within me, as my cognitive understanding of what the Bible says about relationship with God did not match up with my feelings and was outside of my experience. So, now here was another aspect to my Jekyll and Hyde battle: the 'Who is God the Father?' battle.

In recent years I once heard Guy Miller[2] say in a sermon, 'Apostolic doctrine has to be experienced as well as understood', and this sums up where I was; understanding something but not experiencing it.

---

[2] An apostolic leader within the Newfrontiers group of churches. Quote used with permission.

I hadn't experienced being fathered at any meaningful level; now God was breaking in to my understanding that there was more to appropriate. It wasn't enough to read the truth with cognitive understanding, I had to appropriate it, to experience it and to walk in it.

So, though I was still very, very frightened of God, who with a word or a breath could punish me or send me to hell for eternity, I began to slowly recognise that the 'real truth' rather than my 'felt truth' was very different. Yet, I still couldn't seem to really get hold of it. I tried all the suggestions of writing out pertinent texts, sticking them all over the house and reading them aloud every time I saw them. I told myself over and over that the Bible was true, but it all seemed so distant and nothing seemed to go in. It just wasn't working.

Sometimes we can get bogged down with trying to '*live by* the Word' as opposed to having a living relationship '*with* the Word'. God was drawing me towards a deeper relationship with Him, to know Him as Father, yet I was just trying to memorise words on a page. I later began to realise that memorising the words and trying to grapple with truth only has reality when it comes out of a relationship with Him, which makes it all worth grappling for. Truth is not empty words on a page, truth is 'the Word' (John 1:1), Jesus, made alive through the words on the page by the Holy Spirit at work within us.

The fact that I was still regularly erupting like a volcano scared me. I also didn't know why it only ever happened behind closed doors with Stuart when we were alone; it never happened with anyone else. Looking back, I suppose the reason for that was because he was the only one that I felt safe with, without actually realising that at the time. He was the only one who had never, ever, mistreated me. He was the only one who had never said a bad word against me. He was the only one who was always there for me in real life. He was the only one who protected me. So, I suppose without realising it or acknowledging it, I felt a degree of safety with him. Maybe something in me was testing him. Did he really care? Did he really love me? Would he one day end up being abusive? Because I couldn't 'feel' that emotion of love and so could not comprehend how he could love me, maybe I needed to give him reason to walk away. Who knows what was going on deep below the surface, but I do know that I constantly accused him of not caring, not loving me. If you had to describe my behaviour then and were to say, 'This is what she's really like…' to any one of the people who were around us at that time, they probably would not have believed you. They would not have believed that I ever had these eruptions. And Stuart never told a soul.

So that was my pattern of behaviour right from the start of married life: innumerable outbursts followed by a long walk to the point of exhaustion and then a catatonic state followed by several days of sleep. After the sleep I would pray and would confess it all to God – again – and say sorry – again – and ask God to help me – again. And then I'd end up doing it all – again.

The other thing that continued happening in daily life from the point of getting married was this struggle to make any kind of choice. We had a three-bedroom terraced house and I would clean it from top to bottom every day after getting home from work because I was still living with the mindset that I'd had in my parents' house. So, a lot of the time I was exhausted. Stuart used to say, 'You don't have to do all that, you can choose not to do it.' But I couldn't, I could not choose not to do it.

Without processing it in my brain, I think something deep down in me thought that if I didn't clean the house then Stuart would beat me. Because if I didn't do it at my parents' home I'd get beaten, so if I didn't do it in my marital home, I'd get beaten by my husband. He never gave me any cause to think that, but it was in my head; I think it was in my psyche.

When you are subjected constantly to violence and control, then it is that which will write the script in your thinking. Violence brings trauma and fear, putting you constantly in 'survive mode'. Control brings a different kind of fear, fear of the unknown, 'What may happen if…?' It robs you of being able to weigh a matter, to judge the options; it robs you of your ability to make a decision, because you have no ability to trust in your own judgement. And so I simply allowed the lies that had set themselves up within me to reign. I didn't even realise that I could choose anything in life, as I didn't see any other options. I was blinkered into doing what the 'script' in my head had set up within me.

Going to the shops was still hard because people wouldn't serve me. Therefore, as far as possible, Stuart would have to come with me or would have to do it himself. But it wasn't always easy for him to go on his own because he wasn't very capable in terms of cooking and the whole kitchen department! Although I could get something to eat, I didn't really know how to properly cook either. From the choosing what to have through to the preparing of a menu, I didn't know how. So, for example, you might decide that you were going to have lasagne for your evening meal and therefore you would need a list of certain ingredients. I didn't think like that because when we had Domestic Science I was never sent to school with the necessary ingredients. I would therefore always be given the task of cleaning the oven whilst everyone else made biscuits or other tasty things. (I was good at cleaning!) At my parents' home, the things that I made to eat were done on the basis of: 'Well, there's this in the cupboard, so we'll eat this…' If there was a tin of beans and bread, we'd have beans on toast. Or if there were some bananas and bread, we'd have a banana sandwich. So, I couldn't really cook. I didn't know what to do.

I felt that I had to have a food cupboard with at least all the staple items in it. My mother never fed us properly half the time. I remember seeing in the cupboard things like salt, weird things like random spices, baking powder and so on, some things that were probably in the cupboard for months. There were never things like flour, sugar, bread or fresh vegetables around, just a few tinned goods such as evaporated milk, baked beans, peaches and tomatoes. These tinned items and a few spices were then the things I thought should be in my cupboard because I was following the 'script'.

Somewhere during the 1960s, there was the beginning of a reformation happening in the way people shopped for groceries. No longer did you go in and ask the shopkeeper for an item, now there were supermarkets where you went in and had a seemingly vast array of goods in front of you (though they were still small by today's standards!). You would choose what you wanted off the shelves and then you paid somebody on the way out. So, there had been this shift from where you'd go into a shop and ask for beans or salt, to the beginning of supermarket shopping where you'd independently choose things for yourself.

As an older child, when mother told me to go to a shop to get beans, I'd just go and say, 'Beans!' I never said, 'Can I have a tin of beans?' But they got to know me, they knew I didn't say much and just gave me a tin. Or, my grandma, who used to smoke, would say, 'Go and get me some more cigarettes!' (they used to sell them to kids back then) so I'd go and give them the money and say, 'Park Drive!' (a leading brand at the time) and then would take them back to Grandma.

By the time that I had to shop for myself as a married person, I had to venture into the new supermarkets. It wasn't appropriate to say 'beans' anymore, I had to go and find the beans myself. However, unfortunately for me, there were Heinz beans, HP beans, Crosse & Blackwell beans, beans in tomato sauce, beans with this, beans with that. I didn't know what to do!

And this kind of frustration and inability to choose was sparking off the volcano eruption inside of me more and more. What would happen was that I'd go into the shop and I would be alright if there was only one thing to choose. However, if there were a few options in front of me I'd feel paralysed and wouldn't be able to go any further, and then I'd get this great sense of frustration inside me. I'd end up going and paying for what I'd already got and then would run home. When I'd get home I'd be in this really hyped-up state and as soon as Stuart came in, the volcano would erupt. It may sound strange, but the first time I had an actual breakdown was in front of the baked beans section in the local supermarket.

My recollection of it was that I was looking at the beans, completely at a loss as to which ones to buy, and the next thing I knew I was at home in bed. I remembered nothing in-between and still don't to this day. What had apparently happened was that I'd been looking at the beans, and looking at the beans, and looking at the beans, eventually becoming completely catatonic and then somebody had come along and tried to talk to me, but nobody had been able to get through to me because I had totally switched off and disassociated. I had become some kind of non-functioning, robotic person which nobody could get through to. I think on the first occasion the police took me home. On another occasion Stuart had been called, collected me and took me home and then on other occasions it actually happened at home. I had at least three 'nervous breakdowns', as it was then called, that were as bad as the beans episode.

The same thing happened after each breakdown: I went to bed and went to sleep. And I slept for days. I would sleep for far longer than the length of time that I'd sleep after I'd had a volcano eruption: it would literally be for days, and then for weeks I would have to spend much of the day asleep before coming back into living more normally. During this time, there was virtually no getting up, no functioning. Stuart would give me a drink and I'd be taken to the toilet, but it was like I was on some kind of automatic pilot and so I'd go straight back to sleep again. The doctor would rack up the antidepressants and tranquillisers and prescribe even higher doses until I got through it.

Then one day I'd wake up and realise where I was and slowly I would get back into things, and life would go on. And after a period of time I'd get to the same place again and the whole pattern would repeat and carry on. So, over a period of about seven years, that was my oscillating life. And yet in-between all this, I had amazing times with God and the Holy Spirit. I suppose the reason for that was because my times with God were not based on how I felt, they superseded my negative feelings – and the Man in the Picture had always been there.

Throughout my childhood and into my adult life I obviously had regular visits to see the doctor. On one occasion when I visited the surgery it was a different doctor; a locum. He asked me about my state of mind because he could see that every time I came in, all that happened was that I was given more and more pills and now I was due for a repeat prescription. This particular doctor, however, decided that he wasn't going to give me that repeat. He said that this state I was in was not about pills but it was about 'unresolved conflicts'.

That was the first time I'd ever heard that term and the first time ever that someone had suggested to me that there was an underlying root cause for my difficulties. I left his office feeling very disturbed and wondering how on earth I was going to get through without the pills. I thought about what he had said but I didn't know exactly what he meant. I looked it up in the dictionary but I didn't have any sense of any unresolved issues, I was too detached to see anything. So, whilst it was an interjection into everything, it didn't at that point prove to be helpful in any way because I had no idea what that meant for me, so I moved on and the cycle moved into repeat. Because I had not been given a repeat prescription, I got bad again quickly; really bad.

We were so alone, so cut off from anyone who seemed to care about us. The churches around wouldn't have us, neither did we have people around us who we felt we could confide in. I was often setting out walking for miles, just taking off anywhere, walking over the moors that were nearby, walking and walking whilst trying to get my head to stop its constant taunts and commands to end it all. By this point Stuart was desperate to find help, so he contacted the leader of the church that he'd been at prior to the one where he'd met me, the Baptist church.

The leader came to see us. Because we weren't welcome anywhere locally, for those few years we'd just been having our own little times on Sundays. We'd gone off and foraged into other places but nothing had come of it, so this church leader suggested that we needed fellowship, people around us, and that we should consider actually moving house and living nearer his church – in a suburb of Sheffield.

This would mean a move of about eight miles out of our home town, but then we could maybe have a fresh start and attend and become members of that church; also, everyone there already knew Stuart. So we said that we'd go along for a few weeks to see how we felt.

We began travelling to this church every week for a few Sundays. The very first Sunday that we attended there wasn't much outwardly going on to do with the gifts of the Spirit, not much evidence of what we would now call a 'charismatic church'. It was very much a typical Baptist church of its day, at the time what I called a 'hymn sandwich church'; you sang a hymn, sat down, somebody did a reading and then you stood and sang another hymn and so on. But nevertheless, the minute I walked into that place I knew I heard God audibly say, 'This is where I want you to be.' It was the same voice that I had heard speak to me that first week from the book of Jeremiah, yet if anything, even clearer. I looked around to check that someone hadn't spoken those words but there was no one behind me. God had spoken – the Man in the Picture.

Even after going through the service, all in its traditional form, no worship songs (or 'choruses', as we called them then), no hands in the air, no outward demonstrations of the spiritual gifts in operation, my sense that this was the right place to be was so strong that we decided straight away that we would join this church together. I felt these people were all real Christians, and later we discovered that some had already experienced the baptism in the Spirit. We were destined to become a lively, Spirit-filled church.

Chapter Thirteen: A Great Exchange

We moved house and began the task of settling in to a new area. It was hard because we were both from a very parochial, closed-in kind of small town, one that most folk never left but lived there for their whole lives. Now we had pulled out of that, which gave us additional difficulties, with travelling to work and family and so on all still within our home town. And I didn't get a whole lot better.

The fact that we'd moved away from the whole problem of interacting with people and of being called a 'witch' didn't seem to make a lot of difference. Yet now it did mean that I could go to the shops anytime I wished by myself, I could go to the bank myself, I could go anywhere in the area and people would serve me and they wouldn't cross the road when they saw me – simply because they didn't know who I was.

There was definitely a sense of relief moving there, but a lot of very difficult things carried on as usual. I still had trouble trying to make choices. So, once we'd got a particular brand of beans, that was the only one that I would ever buy. I still had the volcanic eruptions and rages, and I still seemed to need to go off for long walks.

The leader of the church was aware of some of my struggles and really wanted to help. He and his wife would sometimes sit with me and pray for me when I was despairing. But I don't think they really knew what to do or how to help me, so I began to go for counselling, through a Christian counselling organisation. I went every single week without missing a session because I wanted to be different, I wanted to be free; most of all, I wanted to be 'normal'.

During that time, I'd left my job in my home town and now had a new job, in Sheffield, which I did enjoy. I did all the elements of the job myself from beginning to end, a complete process – I didn't have to have much interaction with others at all, so it proved to be a good job for me at that time. Another positive about it was that I discovered there was a Christian lady working in another office near to mine. This particular lady had suspected that I was also a Christian, so occasionally she would insist that we had coffee together. This became a hugely important God-appointed relationship because at some point after that, a whole host of things happened that both reinforced me in my walk with God, but also intensified my fight with *Nemo*.

All around that time of my early relationship with this lady, Marjorie, it seemed that every possible distress was flung at us. We were told categorically we would never have children, I began to suffer agonising bouts of pain in my back, Stuart lost his job in the declining steel industry and the final biggest distress of all was the tragic loss of both of Stuart's parents within six weeks of each other. Life had become even grimmer. Though my in-laws had not been in my life very many years, they had become the nearest thing I'd ever had to 'normal' parents. They had taken me into their hearts and loved me despite me being unable to properly reciprocate. That loss was confusing to me as I felt I had to be strong for Stuart, yet losing new-found parental figures affected me profoundly; it became the point where I was finally beginning to completely fall apart.

During that time, I was learning to lean heavily upon God. He was my only solace and my only hope; the Man in the Picture was there in my every waking moment, yet the rage intensified and the cycle of destructive behaviour became even more frequent. On one occasion when I'd had one of these rages, I got to the point of feeling the need to end the exhausting cycle of the battle in my head and found myself thinking: 'I think my mother is right, I'm mentally ill and I do need a doctor. But I don't know what to do about it because nearly two years of weekly counselling and a lifetime of strong drugs do not seem to be working and on top of that, I'm harming Stuart.'

I dwelt for a long time on the harm I was causing him and then made the decision, 'I need to leave Stuart for his sake, and I need to go to the local psychiatric hospital and tell them that I need help.' So, I went to work the next day feeling very downhearted. Marjorie noticed that I was looking even more unhappy than usual and asked me what the matter was. I told her that I had not been 'right' for a long time and had realised that I was mentally ill and that I needed to leave Stuart and voluntarily go to this psychiatric hospital. She then said to me: 'Well, before you do that, would you consider coming to stay with me for a couple of weeks?'

I did; she talked me into it. I went to stay with Marjorie for a couple of weeks or so. I had told Stuart that I was going to leave him as I was damaging him and that I was going to go to the hospital. Obviously, he didn't want me to leave and so was hugely grateful that Marjorie had invited me to stay with her.

Whilst staying with her she took me to her local Anglican church, where she introduced me to a Church Army officer and his wife and asked me whether I would talk with them. I agreed, though I didn't know what to say or how to communicate anything very well.

The couple attempted to ask me lots of questions in order to get to the bottom of my troubles, such as, 'What was your relationship with your parents like? How did you get on with them?' And my answer was always a usual 'Fine'. The reason I said 'fine' wasn't because I was lying. It was because I really did not realise that my life at home, my relationship with my parents, everything at school, was in any way outside of normal. I didn't realise that it wasn't fine. I didn't realise that other people did not have similar childhood experiences, except there was this niggling thought that I'd been having about the fact that I'd never seen Stuart's parents angry with him. I'd seen them a bit irritated with him at times, but I'd never heard his mother call him names and I never saw his father get angry with him. That was bothering me a little bit by this time, but I didn't know why. I didn't realise that something different was being modelled to me.

So, this loving, well-meaning Church Army couple couldn't help me very much at all. Not only did I not answer anything which gave them any clues, but also all of my answers were monosyllabic because I still didn't really speak much. If they asked an open-ended question, we were stuck because I didn't know what to say! In the end they simply said that they'd pray for me before I left. And it proved to be the best thing that they did.

During that time of prayer, nothing happened to me but the lady said that she'd had a vision. She described the vision as seeing a big chain with two hands that had got hold of the chain at both ends. The hands then started to pull the chain so that it came apart in the middle, leaving a broken link on one side. Then one of the hands came and got hold of the broken link and fashioned it so that the broken link was mended. And that was the end of the vision.

Her husband said something like, 'I think that I know what that means. It seems to me the chain is your family line. The hands are the hands of God and He is pulling apart the chain of your family line, until it breaks apart. Where it breaks apart with the broken link, you're the broken link. The hand that comes is God's hand coming to mend the broken link. And then there are two chains: one chain is your family line up to you and that is now finishing, and the other chain is the one that includes you as the link having been mended; that chain is the beginning of a new chain that starts with you. It is a new line of faith.'

It was all very interesting – no one had ever shared anything like that with me before. However, at the time it meant absolutely nothing to me! I didn't understand it. I didn't know what that could mean or what it had to do with what I was going through. I was just still so disassociated, I couldn't interpret it.

We finished the session and I never saw them again, I just saw them that one time. But I never forgot what had happened nor what had been said during that time; it stayed in my mind – 'the mending of a broken link and a new chain, a new line of faith.' Looking back, that was actually to prove to be a pivotal moment, the beginning of the old chain being broken and something new beginning.

After my stay with Marjorie, I returned home to Stuart and went back into work as usual; I didn't leave Stuart or present myself at the hospital. Life continued in much the same vein for a while longer, but in addition, my physical health was deteriorating, particularly the spine, firstly in the neck and then the lower spine and legs. This eventually proved to be the result of all the abuse and trauma, although at that stage it hadn't been diagnosed. So, on the one hand, I'd escaped from the daily onslaught of the abuse from my father, yet on the other hand the consequences of that abuse were still there to have to live with, and at that point still hadn't actually fully manifested themselves.

I started to have times where I would have to lie flat on my back because my neck had locked up and there would be nothing that I could do about it. Over time it progressed into problems with the lower back. These problems started at an early age and had got worse; I remember doing a paper round when I was about thirteen years old when one day I got to a point where I literally couldn't walk. I couldn't get my legs to go where I wanted them to go. So, Mother had to take me to the doctor again. The trouble was, she would take me to the doctor and complain about me not doing things such as not speaking, and then not walking, but still, of course, she would never say, 'Oh, and we also beat her black and blue last night.' So, the doctor only had what he had in front of him to go on. He therefore decided that it was a combination of what used to be called 'growing pains' in my legs and the psychological state that I was in, which he thought meant I wasn't wanting to walk! 'It will all eventually right itself,' he said, whilst dispensing yet more drugs which numbed my brain. But he was wrong; they were all wrong.

I actually had a damaged spine and this didn't get better, nor was it properly diagnosed, until I was about thirty years old. It turned out that my spine was broken in at least three places and was pressing on the nerves in my legs. The right leg in particular was irretrievably damaged because the vertebrae were not stable. But as a child none of that was known; it was 'growing pains'. This led to other subsidiary problems and by the time I was thirty I had become disabled. The pressure from the damaged bone had affected the main nerve to the right leg to the point that I no longer had any sensation in the leg or foot. I had slowly become housebound other than for a painful trip out in the car every Sunday to join the rest of the church in worship. I eventually had major surgery to fuse and pin the spine, which helped a little.

Alongside all these health issues was my struggle with the episodes of the volcano blowing up and the deep blackness of suicidal depression. This is what the person Stuart had married was like!

In later life, as we have travelled together in ministry, when Stuart has been asked about his side of the story – 'How can you go everywhere and just stand by in the background, how do you cope with that?' – the number one thing he always says is, 'Because I heard God on the first night we ever met.' And that's what held him through all the difficulties: 'This is my wife; this is the woman that I love and look after. I could see what God had planned.' Of course, at the time I couldn't actually see any of that plan for myself.

At that point in time, *Nemo* ruled more than ever. 'I can't be healthy because I am a nobody, I don't matter. I can't have children because I am not fit to be a parent and I am not worthy of having a normal life. I am nobody, so it doesn't matter that I can't do this and I can't do that…' *Nemo* was the cause of everything and the reinforcing consequence of everything – seemingly, anyway – and the further difficult issues of life were now accentuating it.

However, God was at work and I clearly remember one particular evening. Stuart was working a night shift and so I was home alone.

I had this experience whereby I think I had fallen asleep, but I still don't really know. In my sleep I was dreaming about Jesus; they had just whipped His back and then put Him on the cross. I saw Him up there, heaving Himself up and down, trying to breathe. His arms were stretched out, pinned to the cross – it wasn't a nice piece of planed wood, it was some old tree. As He was heaving Himself up and down trying to breathe, I was seeing His back, which had already been cut through because He'd been whipped; it was like His flesh started to fall off. The dream was becoming like a nightmare as I somehow locked into the physical pain of what was happening to Him in this dream.

John 12:32 says, 'And I, if I be lifted up from the earth, will draw all men unto me' (AKJV). In the dream I looked at this horrible scene and I felt Jesus' pain because I had pain myself; I was identifying with His pain. I then woke up with my arms stretched out wide. I wondered, 'What was all that about?' and so I started to pray. I then felt God say to me that because of what Jesus went through, 'There has been a great exchange. I have exchanged death for life. Pain and sorrow will be exchanged. There's a great exchange to come. I can heal the spirit of a man [a person], his mental torment, and his physical body.'

I can't remember all the different words, but I knew in that moment that He was saying to me that He hadn't just saved me from my sin, but that He could rescue me from all this battling with *Nemo*. He could rescue me from my mental torment He could heal me from my physical pain. I knew too that I wanted to see others set free and healed in spirit, mind and body. I had to learn to pray for the sick, to expect Him to move in healing on people's bodies, to expect Him to release people from mental torment and to see people brought into His kingdom. And that was the end of that interaction with God.

Somewhere over the next few days I ended up having another one of the volcanic eruptions. I was starting to get really weary of them:

'I don't know how to be different, I don't know how to escape them.' I could tell that I was on the way to yet another breakdown; something in me could tell by now that it was getting to that point again. I just didn't know what to do.

By this time, we'd been married for getting on for eight years – all of this had been going on for nearly eight years. Anyway, I went to Ray, the leader of the church at the time, and said: 'I know I'm getting bad again, but I don't know what to do.'

He prayed with me and I went home. But Ray had also got to the point where he didn't know what to do, either. So, he contacted some friends in another church in the south of England and spoke to someone there, and basically it was decided that I needed to go and see this person. Ray came back to me and said that he thought it would be a good idea for me to go to stay with some friends of his at this other church. I somewhat cynically said, 'What do mean, so that they can sort me out? Well, actually, whatever will help, I don't care anymore.' So, I went to stay with people who I'd never met before.

Chapter Fourteen: Broken Chains

I was really nervous because I'd never stayed with people I didn't know before. I didn't know how to interact with them; I didn't know what to say and I felt awkward having my meals with them. I actually remember stabbing myself in the mouth with my fork because I was so nervous of being with them and eating with them at mealtimes! They were just my hosts and the plan was that I would then go and meet this other man to see what he had to say.

I went to see the man and the scenario was actually very similar to going to see the Church Army officer and his wife – there were lots of questions. Again I was asked, 'How did you get on with your parents?' and again I said, 'Fine.' He asked me other questions like that to which I just responded, 'Fine' and 'I don't know', in my usual way. He must have felt frustrated because he seemed a bit offhand towards me; I thought perhaps this was because he didn't know how to get me to speak or converse. At the end of that consultation, which was only about half an hour, he said: 'I can see that this is becoming a waste of time. You are so obviously in need of deliverance.'

I knew what deliverance meant in terms of the biblical context, but I didn't know what it meant outside of the biblical stories. By this point it was the beginning of 1980 and in the north of England 'charismatic' things such as speaking in tongues were only just starting to happen a little more widely. So, I didn't really know what 'deliverance' meant in its practical sense. The only references I'd heard to it was from all the wrong things that people had been saying about me a few years earlier and from what I'd heard about *The Exorcist* film. I'd never actually seen *The Exorcist*, but I knew that the rumours which people had spread about me had said things like, if I put my hands on people their head would go around in a circle, or that if I put my hands on people they would turn green and be sick, that sort of thing. In the Bible I'd read about the Gadarene demoniac where the demons were sent into the pigs; there it only said that once he'd had deliverance he was 'in his right mind' (Luke 8:35) but I didn't feel as though I was totally 'out of my mind'. I therefore didn't know how to interpret that term, although I'd heard about it and read about it in the Gospels.

Nevertheless, the man said, 'You are so obviously in need of deliverance, you just need to be set free from a spirit of…' And then he came out with a list, one thing after the other – 'rejection, anger, fear, torment, occult demons, control, violation, suicide…' and it carried on. It was such a long list that I just sat there and looked at him blankly. When he'd finished, he asked me a question: 'By the way, did your mother lose a child before she had you?'

'No,' I replied.

'Oh, and there's occult practices in your family, isn't there?' he added.

I did know what that meant, so I said, 'No, there isn't!' as up to that point I was unaware of anything at all.

He then said, 'Well, I'm not getting anywhere, am I? If you have no faith, then there's no point in me praying. You go away and if you change your mind and find the faith, come back.'

I went away really upset. I was taken aback by the things he had said; I wanted to try to 'find faith' but it really couldn't be that easy, could it?

Sometimes we grapple with difficulties for so long that we find it hard to believe that God can set us free. We feel as I did: 'It can't be that simple, can it?' But it *is* that simple; it is about putting our trust in God alone and allowing Him to work. It's not even about us having to find some extra level of faith, or find *anything* within ourselves to effect that freedom; it is about trusting that God can do what He has said He can do.

I felt as though I'd got to the end of myself and I could see that others had got to the end of themselves with me as well. I didn't know how to break out of it. Ray had sent me to be with his friends and this was, it felt like, my last chance. But then it hadn't gone very well at all because I couldn't talk with this man; that's what it felt like to me. I came away from that meeting thinking, 'I don't know what to do.' I was so upset because I felt like it wasn't that I didn't have faith, it was just that I didn't know how to interact with the man. And the whole list of things he said I needed to be delivered from – I just didn't understand what all of that was about.

I felt totally overwhelmed by it all; the realisation that I'd become a real problem to others even when they were trying to help me, the years of battling, the trauma and the pain of living with the results of what others had done...

Then the whole *Nemo* thing kicked in again: 'Well, it doesn't matter anyway, I'm *Nemo*, I'm nobody, I don't deserve to be here, I shouldn't be here, I'm nobody, I'm not worth all this effort from everyone.' Then the suicidal voice was replaying again and again, 'Take the tablets, take the tablets' because even then I always carried some in my pockets.

Then I got into even more of a battle because I thought, 'I'm not at home! I can't not be with these people because they'll wonder where I am.' It took all my effort to go back to my hosts' house, but then I couldn't sit with them and eat. I had to go to the room that they were letting me use; I just went straight up there. I had a Bible which was on the floor and I picked it up and looked down at the text where it had randomly opened up. It was Zechariah 9:12. I was still using the Authorized (King James) Version and the way it reads in there is startling. It says: 'Turn you to the strong hold, ye prisoners of hope: even today do I declare that I will render double unto thee'. It was another of those verses that 'stood out on stalks' for me and I thought, 'There is yet hope!' I then accidentally dropped the Bible and so I picked it up again and exactly the same thing happened.

This time it opened at Isaiah 61. Verses 1-3 read:

> The Spirit of the LORD GOD *is* upon me;
> because the LORD hath anointed me to preach good tidings unto the meek;
> he hath sent me to bind up the brokenhearted,
> to proclaim liberty to the captives,
> and the opening of the prison to them that are bound;
> to proclaim the acceptable year of the LORD,
> and the day of vengeance of our God;
> to comfort all that mourn;
> to appoint unto them that mourn in Zion,
> to give unto them beauty for ashes,
> the oil of joy for mourning,
> the garment of praise for the spirit of heaviness …

Again, the Authorized (King James) Version at the time really seemed to impact me deeply.

Further along it says: 'For your shame ye shall have double' (AKJV); the NIV reads: 'Instead of your shame you will receive a double portion' (v. 7). When I read the earlier bit about 'beauty for ashes, the oil of joy for mourning, the garment of praise for the spirit of heaviness' (or 'spirit of despair', NIV), it reminded me of my experience not many weeks earlier when God had spoken to me about a great exchange. I kept looking at the passage and reading 'instead of this, there will be that'; truly a great exchange. I then felt as though something subsided inside of me and I desperately wanted that man to pray, even though I didn't understand what he had said or what was happening and didn't know what 'deliverance' would involve.

That Sunday morning, I went to my hosts' church meeting and in the middle of the worship time I had an 'open vision'. What I mean by that is that I didn't have my eyes shut, they were open and so although I was seeing the words of the song as I was singing, I also started to see something else beginning to be superimposed over that. I saw a dog chained up to a pole. The dog was running around and around the pole until it couldn't move at all because it had got the chain wrapped around the pole so much. Then I saw a hand come down and unclip the chain from the dog collar and the dog ran free. And in that moment, I just knew that the dog was me. I was just like the dog, in that I couldn't move anywhere, and I thought, 'I've got to get that man to pray with me.' God had given me a sense of faith; I felt different; something had happened in my spirit that gave me a certainty that He was going to set me free.

I told the people that I was staying with, 'I need that man to pray with me. I need him to know that I need him to pray.' They were very reassuring and said, 'Don't worry, we will take you back.' So, they took me back to the man. I still couldn't talk to him very much, but I did manage to get through to him that I did want him to pray. He therefore arranged a time, got another person to be with him and the two of them prayed for me.

Now, the big question I often get asked is, 'Can a Christian be "possessed" by a demon?' The word used in the Bible, such as in Luke 4:33, comes from the root *daimonizomai* (δαιμονίζομαί), which is Greek, meaning in our modern-day language, as near as we can get, 'to be possessed by a demon'. But if we are Christians, surely we who belong to God cannot be 'possessed'?

Sometimes maybe from our pre-Christian life or perhaps from something we have been opened up to, as in my case, there can be a particularly strong battle because a demon has gained an entry into our life. That demon cannot 'possess' me but it can unduly influence me, cause me to stay in dark places, cause me to think, feel and act in ways that are unhealthy and prevent me growing in God. That demon can cause such a strong hold on me that I am in that sense 'under the power or influence of' a demon. It's a bit like having a physical illness. I am fully alive but because I'm under the power of an illness, I am struggling, and even sometimes need medicines to help me to get rid of that illness. Then after medication, I am 'delivered' from the illness and set free to get on with life.

Though the enemy may have gained some strongholds in our lives via demons gaining an entry at some point, or through repeated patterns of thinking that have built up, he cannot possess us at the core of our being. At the core of our being, our spirit has been made alive in Christ, fully alive, fully light, fully 'hidden with Christ in God' (Colossians 3:3), so in that sense nothing can possess us, as now we belong to God.

What then happens is that new life, that light will permeate through the rest of our being, the psyche, the mind, the emotions and even the physical body, to gradually bring more light and more freedom to our whole being. This is why for some people it seems that problems that were coped with before becoming a Christian seem to get worse after becoming a Christian. It means that the Holy Spirit is now at work to change us 'from one degree of glory to another' (2 Corinthians 3:18, ESV) and the darkness is now being challenged so that we can be set free.

The day I was prayed for I wasn't afraid, I was just desperate to be free, and yet at the same time I found it hard to believe that one prayer could change things so much. But then, I thought to myself, 'Just one prayer brought me into a new life with God, so maybe this one prayer can now break something in me. I believe that this is the moment; the moment the hand of God will come and release the chain that has trapped me for so long.'

At the start of the session they explained to me their approach. 'This is what we're going to do. We're going to pray for you and we're going to tell these various things to go, in Jesus' name. We are speaking to the demons, not to you.' And that's just what happened. The prayer time lasted about twenty minutes, they did not perform any weird or ritualistic ceremonies, nor jump around or even loudly shout; they simply spoke with authority as they told things to leave in the name of Jesus. And I didn't go green and my head didn't spin around and I wasn't sick and I didn't cough! In fact, I hardly discerned anything happening at all.

I can't remember exactly what they told to go, it was a very long list, but it included rejection, self-rejection, fear, violation, torment, control and suicide. At some point they also spoke to 'anger' and when they did that, I just briefly felt like pushing them away, because they both had gently laid a hand on each of my shoulders. Other than that, I felt nothing.

When they got to the end of their prayers, they asked me, 'How do you feel? What did you feel?' to which I replied, 'Well, I didn't really feel anything!' They didn't quite seem to believe me and said, 'What, nothing at all?'

So I told them, 'Well, when you prayed about anger I felt a little bit like I just wanted to push you off.'

Then the man I'd originally spoken with said, 'Oh, that's easy. We need to pray about anger that's directed towards others as well as that directed towards you.' Where he got that equation from, I still do not know, but that's what he said! So they then prayed for that. However, when he said 'Amen' that time, something did happen.

When they said 'Amen', it felt like all my life, up to that moment, I'd had a very, very tight elastic band going right down the middle of my body, pulled very, very tight, and everything was based on that tightness right down the middle of my body. When they said 'Amen', it felt like the elastic band snapped. I felt completely different and somehow a little scared by the feeling, but mostly it felt strange and good not to have that tightness going right through me. What I later realised was that for the first time in my life I was experiencing what it felt like to relax.

I had finally relaxed! I was twenty-six years old at that point and I'd never felt the experience of relaxation until then. Since that moment I've experienced it a lot more, and I've experienced tension again as well, so I know that's what it was; the moment for the first time in my life that I had ever felt relaxed.

So, at that point I knew that God had done something significant in me, although I didn't know exactly what He'd done. The chain had been pulled apart and a link had been broken. That was the end of what seemed like 'part one' of my deliverance.

Chapter Fifteen: The Presence of the Spirit

I came back home and told Ray that I'd had this prayer, and described to him what had happened, with this feeling of the elastic band breaking (the experience of relaxation). I told him that as a result of that I knew that God had done something. I also told him about the things the man had asked me, about occult practices in the family and whether my mother had had a child before me, and that I'd said, 'No.' I also told him about how he'd prayed about this, that and the other spirit. So, I came back to Sheffield with a sense that God had done something big, but I didn't yet know quite what He had done. And I still didn't have any understanding of my background as being anything other than normal.

Immediately after returning to Sheffield on my first night home I had a dream. The dream was of a real incident which had happened at school; a bullying episode. I was in the classroom. It was a class where the teacher wasn't really in control of the pupils; he was getting ready to retire. The way he taught religious instruction was that he used to open the Bible, put his head down and start reading it for a solid hour. Or similarly, for history, he would attempt to get us all to try to perfect the drawing of woolly mammoths, and those would be the lessons! In the meantime, while he had his head down reading the Bible, there would be utter chaos at the back of the classroom, which he seemed able to totally ignore – he would just carry on reading until the end of lesson bell rang. No one was really interested in his lessons at all. However, on this particular occasion, I was sitting, bored just like everyone else, but then I started to smell a horrendous smell, a burning smell.

The next thing I knew the boys behind me started battering me on the head. They had thought that it would be funny to set my hair alight with a cigarette lighter but it had taken hold and that's what the burning smell was. That had then frightened them and so they were hitting me around the head, trying to put it out. Everyone ended up hitting me around the head. They did manage to put out the flames but quite a lot of my hair had already burned away at the back. So, for a long while I walked around with quite a lot of hair missing, or singed.

Anyway, in the dream this incident came back to me. I was reliving it and I could smell the terrible burning and feel the fear from when I was being hit over the head and was thinking, 'What's going on?' Then the dream finished and I woke up. The next day I went to bed and dreamed exactly the same dream. For two weeks, every night, I dreamed the same dream about this event – something that really had happened.

I didn't know what to make of it. It was one isolated event and it wasn't the worst thing that had ever happened to me, by any means. Worse things had happened at home, worse things had happened at school, this was just one random incident; but after two weeks of having this same dream I didn't know what to do about it, and so I went back to see Ray. I told him about the dream and how it had repeated every night for two weeks continuously. 'Maybe we should come around and pray for you about it,' he offered.

I agreed and an appointment was made for him and his wife, Jean, to come to see us so they could try to decide what was going on with this reoccurring dream, and so that they could pray for me. So, they came around on this particular day, two weeks after I'd had the prayer in the south of England.

At the beginning of the prayer time, Ray simply said: 'OK, let's stand together and I'll just pray for the presence of God to be with us as we discuss this.'

We all closed our eyes and Ray began to pray. Nobody was touching me, no one had laid hands on me or anything like that, and no one expected what came next! In the middle of Ray's prayer about God's presence being with us, it felt as if someone had come with their fist and given me an upper cut, just like a boxer does. I was thrown across the room onto the floor, seemingly totally knocked out. It wasn't physically painful like that kind of punch could have been, but it was that powerful in its effect. No one had actually touched me and no one saw anyone or anything touch me. But what they did see was me flying across the room and then me lying flat out on the floor, totally out of it. I was knocked out in the Spirit – literally!

During that time in whatever state I could be thought of as being in, it felt as though I had begun to relive everything that had happened to me when the hair-burning incident occurred. It wasn't simply that I was remembering it; to me I was actually reliving it. I was no longer conscious of being in my living room in any way, I wasn't conscious of everyone there; all I was doing was reliving this event as though it were happening to me in that moment. What I wasn't aware of either was the fact that I was also actually speaking about it as I was reliving it; I was voicing something out loud.

I don't know exactly what I was voicing because all I knew was that I was reliving things, it was all happening *now*, but I was told later that there was a lot of crying and shouting going on. Ray and Jean decided that although they weren't sure what was going on, they obviously needed to pray about this. Stuart told me afterwards that one of them knelt at one side of me, and one of them knelt at the other side, and they literally just prayed. I never heard their prayers but they prayed about whatever it was that I was saying or crying about as it came out.

What then happened for about an hour and a half to two hours was that, just randomly, events came to light about various things that had happened at home and at school; things that had been said and done. There was no order or timeline to it; they were all mixed up together. But one by one all these different memories were coming out of me, almost like some negative stream of consciousness. These things had actually happened and had been locked up somewhere deep inside for all of my life up to that point. It felt like I was locked into a whole series of abusive events, and desperately scrabbling to escape.

Throughout it all, I was talking, crying or screaming about what was happening to me. Ray and Jean were just praying and praying about every single thing that I said, although I didn't hear any of their prayers and I wasn't aware how they were praying. Somewhere before two hours had nearly passed, I started to become more aware of where I was. Ray noticed and said, 'Come on, come on, you've had enough, sit up. Let's get you a drink.'

Ray and Jean then worked at actually getting me out of whatever state I had been in. I was a bit dazed. I wasn't sure what had just happened. They explained to me that I'd said an awful lot of stuff about my past and it was clear to them that it had not been very good at all, and that this was clearly where all my difficulties had stemmed from. Then Ray said, 'I don't think God has finished. You've had enough now, but I don't think God has finished whatever He is doing. We need to pray about all this, but we'll fix another time up for that and we'll come back.'

I waited two weeks for them to return, all the while feeling like I was in some kind of strange limbo waiting for something to finish. Then they came back as promised. Ray said, 'Well, I suggest we talk about what we should do next. But before we start, I want to ask God to be present with us.' So, just like the previous time, we all stood up and Ray began to pray and just like a repeat of the previous time, part way through him praying, not touching me or anything, it felt like I'd been knocked out again and thrown onto the floor and put into a state where I wasn't aware of my surroundings. And then, according to the three of them, I literally started where I'd ended the previous time; I'd finished mid-sentence last time and I literally started from where I left off!

That second time was much deeper, much worse, much more traumatic. I talked about various distressing things to do with what had been done to me at home by my parents and other relatives. There is no need to detail them all here, no need to focus on the depth. And even back then it wasn't that every single happening had to come out; it was more like it just needed a random selection of events to surface in order for the floodgates to open so that something deep inside could be released.

I was sobbing a lot. My understanding now is that I must have been crying so much that it actually affected my blood pressure, because at the time, it felt as though I was passing out in waves; wave after wave of feeling as though I was going to pass out and go somewhere dark, never to come back. Things would go dark – very, very, dark – in those moments, and it was as if I could see the devil himself laughing at me. But then that wave would pass and it would seem like there was a brilliant light waiting for me and I could see the Man in the Picture. I could see Him with His golden glow and a big light and I could see that He was stretching out His arms, waiting for me.

It felt like I oscillated in waves between those two states, darkness and light, all whilst I was heavily crying and unaware of my surroundings. Crying wasn't something that I was ever able to do easily. I wouldn't say I never cried, I could 'well up', but it didn't happen much at all, and it hasn't happened much since. Looking back, I don't think I ever cried as a child; well, not that I can remember, anyway. I think that level of sobbing and crying somehow affected me physically and had an impact on what I was experiencing. It honestly felt like I was teetering on the edge of being totally taken over by the devil, completely going mad, like the man of the Gadarenes.

In those dark moments I would hear mother saying, 'You're mental, you, you need a doctor' and all the different accusations that I'd ever had over my life – 'You're a witch', 'You're evil', 'The very devil himself uses you'. Every one of those things was muddled up in that time.

And then the wave would pass and I'd see the Man in the Picture and the light, and the things that I'd read in the Bible would be there, like, 'you will know the truth, and the truth will set you free' (John 8:32) and Jesus 'came to seek and to save the lost' (Luke 19:10). And I would oscillate between these two places. Somewhere deep inside of me, in that state on the floor, I just knew that I was either going to come out of this completely mad, never able to cope with life again and needing serious help for the rest of my life, or I was going to come out of this totally set free.

What I don't think I realised for a number of years afterwards, was that because I had been disassociated so completely it had never occurred to me that everything that had happened to me wasn't good and it wasn't normal. What therefore seemed to be happening was that some kind of cork was coming out and something was happening that was bringing my personality back together.

That traumatic experience went on for a similar amount of time, about an hour and a half to two hours. Towards the end of this battle, I really knew that I was fighting. I was fighting to come out of this set free and not swallowed up for life with the whole trauma of it all. Again, this experience wasn't just me remembering it; I was reliving it. It wasn't like I was trying to do some kind of guided imagery or trying to go over what had happened imagining that Jesus was by my side and seeing Him in every situation, as some might have suggested should happen according to teachings at that time.[3] No, I was reliving these things. But now, though I didn't realise it, I was talking about them too.

All I knew was, 'This is happening to me right now. Help! Now this is happening to me. Help me!' As I said before, it wasn't a chronological, ordered reliving of my entire past; it was a random set of events that

[3] See for example Ruth Carter Stapleton, *The Gift of Inner Healing* (New York: Bantam Books, 1977).

represented my life. So, in amongst the mix there would be fairly 'mild' things (which still would not seem very good to someone else, but for me they were fairly mild, relatively speaking) and then there were some very, very, traumatic and horrendous things. And they were all muddled up. Apparently, at one point in the first of the two sessions, I'd spoken about Father telling me how worthless and useless I was. His name for me was always 'Stupid idiot' or 'Clumsy clot', so he was telling me how worthless and useless I was. I started saying, 'I'm nobody, I'm nobody, I'm useless, I'm nobody – you can't even look after the cat!'

In the experience that I was going through I was obviously reliving something but Ray and Jean were left scratching their heads, 'What's this about looking after the cat?' They eventually managed to piece together (and I also filled it in for them afterwards) that I was not allowed a pet. My brother and sister were allowed pets so I remember guinea pigs and rabbits being around the place, even goldfish at one time. But I wasn't allowed a pet because I was 'useless' and 'worthless' and couldn't be relied upon to look after a pet. However, one day a ginger tom stray cat came to the house for a while and I used to feed it. I would sit with this cat on my knee and stroke it and talk to it and sometimes in private I would tell it how I felt. My parents laughed at me about my attachment to this cat. Then one day the stray cat didn't come anymore and Father said, 'See, you're totally useless, you can't even look after a stray cat.' The stray was like a cat that had come from nowhere and nobody knew where it belonged and it didn't have a name and it didn't have an identity, and then it went back to nowhere. I felt an affinity with the cat; the cat was a *Nemo*, like me.

This experience involving the cat had arisen in the first session. Towards the end of the second session, when it felt as though blackness was engulfing me and the enemy was laughing at me and I was thinking, 'I'm mad, I'm a witch, I'm useless, I'm worthless, I shouldn't be here' and all that stuff, when that wave passed and I saw the Man in the Picture bathed in light, towards the end of that time I began to see Him holding His arms out to me, and there was a black and white kitten in His arms. Stuart, Jean and Ray could tell that the second session had finished and I could tell it had finished because I went quiet and realised for the second time, 'I'm lying on my living room floor again, it's happened again!'

But this time I felt different. I couldn't tell you how I felt, or what I felt had just happened; I didn't know what to think, but I just felt different. I knew something was finished; the sense of being relaxed was there again and I knew I was finally free.

After the end of the second session I sat up and at first maybe they thought, 'That's it, she's gone mad,' because the first words that came out my mouth were, 'I'm going to have a black and white kitten. God is going to give me a black and white kitten!' We talked for a while and I told them about what I saw at the end and why I thought I was going to get a black and white kitten – because Jesus had had His arms open, holding out to me a black and white kitten.

However, at that point they were unable to carry on talking to me because Stuart, who had had to endure listening to this stuff twice now, was very distraught. I think he found the second part pretty horrendous. He was pacing up and down and wanted to go and find my father and kill him! He was so angry, frustrated and upset. We'd been married nearly eight years at this point and he hadn't heard about any of these things until now. He obviously knew about the time when Father hit me and almost broke my nose because it caused him to bring forward our wedding date, but that was it. So, Ray and Jean then had to spend some time with him, sitting him down, calming him, praying with him and talking to him about forgiveness. They had to switch their ministry to him.

I just sat there that whole time, almost like when you're coming around from an anaesthetic when you're slightly spaced out but you're all relaxed with not a care and you're all OK. I sat there with a mug of tea just aware that something had gone, but not only had something gone, something about *me* was different; but I didn't really know what was different and I didn't know who I was now.

The one thing that I did know was that I was free. I was free! I was still me, but not me! The new me was yet to be discovered!

As I said before, I don't think I realised this for a long time but in hindsight, I think that what had happened in those sessions was that everything that had been suppressed over all those years, everything that had caused me to be totally disassociated, was coming up and out, which therefore meant that at the end of it I was quite a bit more of an integrated person.

Because of how significant that time had been for me, in that moment I made a sort of a pledge to God. I don't want to say 'a vow' because that sounds too strong, but I made a pledge to God while I was there sitting on the floor, a little bit spaced out, and while the others were concerned with Stuart. I just thought that if He could do this for me and set me free, then He could do anything for anybody, and I wanted to help others to be free. I knew in that moment that that's what I wanted to devote my life to; helping others to be free, helping others to be whole, helping others to know God like this.

And that's what I began to do. Over the years I trained in many different aspects of 'people helping', as I call it, and that's what I still try to do. That's why I am writing all of this down, because I want you to know that you can be free too.

I know that neither Ray nor any of one us planned to do what we did or chose the way it all happened, and I don't think we should look for things to happen in this way for others, either. We should just be open to go with what God is doing. I had numerous conversations with Ray and Jean afterwards as we tried to make sense of it all: 'What do you think God was doing? What do you think was happening?' We tried to piece together what we thought God had been doing because none of us had ever seen or heard of anything like that. I certainly wouldn't recommend it as any sort of method that should be replicated! But I would see it as encouragement to trust that God can break into the darkest of situations with His miraculous power to bring freedom and healing.

I also see those sessions as being 'part two' of my deliverance!

Chapter Sixteen:
Release Through Forgiveness

If we are to overcome the enemy's work in our lives and find any freedom, at some point we will come to a place of recognising the need to forgive. When Stuart heard what had happened to me, he became very angry. He wanted to go to my parents and make them suffer for what they had done; he wanted to 'make them pay' for their actions. Sometimes in our anger we can be filled with bitterness that sparks an intention to cause pain. We are then in danger of becoming like one of the perpetrators.

However painful a situation is, we cannot allow ourselves to become overwhelmed like this because all it does is create damage to our own self.

Jesus told a parable about an unmerciful servant in Matthew 18:23-35, who had been forgiven a great debt but tried to exact payment from someone who owed him little. This parable illustrates just how much we have received from God. All our 'debts' have been cancelled, all our sins have been forgiven, there is nothing we can do to repay Him, He has done it all, He has paid the price to set us free. So, how can we not extend that same grace to others? As we are shown in the parable, we are to forgive as we have been forgiven; just as we have received mercy, we are to be merciful. We are not destined to become perpetrators of spiteful revenge; we are destined to be like Jesus, the merciful and forgiving One.

To forgive is not something that depends upon our feelings; if we wait until we feel like forgiving, it will never happen. To forgive is a conscious choice to draw a line under something and move on, to let go of our anger, our hurt, our pain, whatever has been seething inside of us, and treat it as done with. It means releasing our resentment and any desire to 'make them pay', even if it seems the persons don't deserve that forgiveness.

Stuart was able to grapple with this and came to that place of forgiving as I sat on the floor, dazed and drinking tea. For him it was done with and he moved on.

For me, it was much more of a journey. At that point I didn't feel any need for revenge. I didn't feel anything particularly that one could say was vengeful or angry; I was still coming through the letting out of what had been blocked inside from the effects of actual happenings. I was enjoying a new sense of freedom. The battle came later.

After all this had happened, I began a journey of what I call 'walking free'. But that process of choosing to believe something different did mean that I had to also choose to believe that I should forgive; that my faith was not just about having my sins forgiven by God, but that I too had to forgive others in the same way in order for me to fully walk in the freedom I now had. Because it had never occurred to me until now that my life wasn't normal, that the difficulties I have outlined should not have happened, I had never felt any resentment or need to forgive anyone. But now, as I faced up to having lived through a nightmare of different issues, everything came rolling in.

The things that various people in the church in my home town had said and done, the shopkeepers ostracising me, the ones who had wanted to shut me down, Father and his inability to contain his anger and his beatings, but most of all Mother and her strange and manipulative mind games... All of a sudden I felt that I was the guilty one because I wasn't forgiving; I was now the bad guy! But to forgive felt as though I was saying, 'It's OK that you said I was evil, it's OK that you wouldn't serve me, it's OK that you beat me, it's OK that you hated me so much that you locked me away.' How can the one who has been damaged by the sins of others be the one who has to actively forgive? I had lived all my life battling to be free, I was becoming disabled, living with the consequences of what had been done to me, yet now it was down to me, I had to forgive.

It didn't feel possible because I didn't *feel* forgiving. I realised that though the spirit of anger which had been 'cast out' and had so badly affected me, had gone, in that moment there was now another step. I had to choose to forgive. I began with the 'lesser' areas, those who were on the periphery of my 'list', but it took me a long while to get to the point where I could say I had forgiven my father and my mother. I read the parables and sayings of Jesus, and I thought deeply about the 'Lord's Prayer', the prayer I had remembered bits of from school, and especially the line about God forgiving us our sins as we had forgiven those who sinned against us (Luke 11:4). I eventually came to the place of only wanting to have nothing in the way between me and the Man in the Picture. I wanted Him to always be there, and that relationship with Him depended on my forgiving others even as He had forgiven me. So, I made the choice to forgive; it was not based on how I felt, but on the truth I now wanted to walk in every day.

Forgiveness is not about having a change of feeling, it is about letting go of something, drawing a line under it and leaving it. Forgiveness does not mean, 'I am saying that what you did was nothing, it's OK, forget it.' It's not about glossing over things or condoning things in some way that should not have happened. It means that I am taking the knife out of my own heart, I am removing myself from the woundedness of what was in my own soul, I am freeing myself to get on with life without any grudge about what has gone before, but of course I am doing that with the help of God, who first forgave me. Forgiveness releases me far more than it releases the one who has hurt me. Some folk say to me that they admire the way I have 'come to terms' with what happened but my reply is, 'I haven't. There is no coming to terms with child abuse. It should never have happened. But what has been done is forgiven, and now it's gone, it's buried.'

Living with the consequences of what has been done to you doesn't mean you cannot forgive. To forgive releases us from a pit of bottled-up hurt that has the potential to destroy us.

Psalm 32:3 says: 'When I kept silent about my sin, my body wasted away Through my groaning all day long' (NASB). The psalmist, David, is talking here about bottling up his own sin and how that makes him feel like his body is wasting away. Just as surely, as we bottle up our unforgiveness towards others it can affect even our physical health. Today it has been proven that an unforgiving attitude can be at the root of some physical illnesses.[4] Hebrews 12:15 tells us, 'See to it that no one comes short of the grace of God; that no root of bitterness springing up causes trouble, and by it many be defiled' (NASB). When we allow unforgiveness to fester for too long it becomes bitterness, and bitterness eats us away.

Forgiveness is also not about forgetting. Just because I have forgiven does not mean that my mind is blanked and I no longer remember those things. Rather, it means I can remember those things with no ill feeling and, in time, remember without any pain in the remembering. As I write, there is no pain in the recalling of events, though there was at one time, and they should never have happened; nevertheless, those things are past and gone and no longer give me pain. Mother lived well into her eighties and in the last years of her life, I was able to help to take care of her needs and interact with her. I hadn't forgotten, but I had forgiven, and by then she had no power over me anymore; the relationship had changed. I had changed.

Forgiveness doesn't mean the relationship needs to remain the same, or indeed that it should continue. Forgiveness doesn't mean there may not also be a need for justice. But forgiveness helps us far more than we realise; it releases us from continually feeling the pain

---

[4] https://thepsychologist.bps.org.uk/volume-30/august-2017/forgiveness (accessed 3.9.20); https://www.psychologytoday.com/gb/blog/the-couch/201901/forgiving-and-not-forgiving-can-both-affect-your-health (accessed 3.9.20); https://www.counselling-directory.org.uk/memberarticles/unforgiveness-and-your-health (accessed 3.9.20).

and hurt, helps us to let go of those hurts that otherwise would stab at us continually, and it gives us freedom.

If there are things that you have experienced and need to forgive then make the choice, otherwise you're keeping those things as alive as if they were still happening now. You don't have to live with that anymore, it need not be yours.

Chapter Seventeen: Choosing the New

In the two years prior to the deliverance, I had been going to a Christian counsellor, someone whom I respected greatly and was highly respected in his field. Every week I attended for 'non-directive' counselling. I have to say that whilst it was helpful because it gave me a place to offload, it just kept me going for another week; it didn't solve anything, address anything, or bring to light any deep-seated issues. I don't think it could have done, because I was too disassociated.

Deliverance wasn't part of the way the counsellor worked, or necessarily even believed in. After 'part two' of the deliverance I went to his office and shared with him something of what had happened and said, 'I don't need to come for counselling anymore.' He was worried about me. He was very concerned and thought that I should still have counselling, to maybe make a bigger gap between appointments, but that I should still go. But I insisted, 'No, no I don't need to come anymore.'

And I didn't need to, I never went again. Now everything felt different. Everything *was* different. The supernatural intervention of God had plundered the enemy's goods! Over the years, as a Christian, I had tried to take hold of the truth of God's Word. I'd tried to take hold of the fact that 'if anyone is in Christ, the new creation has come: the old has gone, the new is here!' (2 Corinthians 5:17) but I couldn't live in that way and properly grasp it. However, now all kinds of things kicked in almost unnoticeably, from that moment onwards after the end of that second session.

For instance, going to the shops was different. Now I'd go into the shop, I'd look at the vast array of things and I'd look at the baked beans and see the different brands and my mind would think, 'OK, so I've got into this rut of deciding that we only ever have Heinz baked beans, but I don't need to keep having them. I can have something different… ooh, I think I will! I'll have a tin of HP baked beans instead of Heinz!' There was a whole shift in my thinking and I was beginning to recognise that I had a choice. This was being made very, very apparent to me at that time: 'I can choose.' In these early days after my deliverance, I almost felt that at every junction of decision it was as though I could hear the words, 'You can choose.' Many times when I was indecisive, I would hear 'You can choose!' And instead of being immobilised and frozen, I would step out and make a choice.

Things at church were different as well. In my church life, at the end of every meeting there used to be a hubbub of social chitchat, which I previously just could not handle because 'I wasn't meant to be there. I'm no one, I'm invisible'. What would happen previously was that at the end of the message, at the 'Amen' and other closing remarks, I would just whizz out of the door and leave Stuart to do all the socialising; I would go home and get on with fixing up a meal. Well, the very next Sunday after my experience, the sermon finished with an 'Amen' and I got up and then thought: 'You can choose. You don't have to leave now.'

But then *Nemo* kicked in: 'But you do have to leave, you're nobody, you shouldn't be here, you don't belong in your family and you don't belong in the church family.' But then I thought, 'No! No, I'm going to stay for five minutes.'

I sat in the pew and timed myself: exactly five minutes, during which I had to listen to all the old rubbish in my head: 'You don't belong here, you shouldn't be here, you're invisible, you're no man, you're nobody, you're *Nemo*.' But then I also found myself speaking back to that voice by saying to myself, 'But God has put me here; he has adopted me into this family. These are my brothers and sisters. I belong in His family. He chose me to be here before the foundation of the world. I belong here.' It was like I was having a conversation with this other part of myself that had ruled all this time – and it was jolly hard work! As soon as five minutes had finished, I shot out of the building. I did that for a number of weeks: five minutes exactly. But then I thought that actually I was dealing with five minutes pretty well, so I decided to do ten minutes!

What I didn't realise at the time was the importance of what I was doing: I was combating the *lies* that came from the enemy with God's *truth.* And as I did that, I began to walk free; the power of the truth was at work in me to transform me by the renewing of my mind (Romans 12:2). I didn't realise I was speaking scriptures to myself that were key to my coming away from the lies. No one taught me to do that but I was remembering scriptures such as those in Romans 8:14-17, Ephesians 1:3-6 and related passages such as Psalm 139:15-16. All I knew was that I was timing myself ten minutes, week after week, choosing to stay around despite how I was feeling; until that somewhat horrendous day when, during that ten minutes, someone actually came and sat next to me and tried to have a conversation – now, that was a bit sticky! But it was the beginning of a breakthrough; the beginning of being able to take my place within a body of believers and know them as my family.

Church is many things, a temple, a body, an army and so on, but it is also family. He 'sets the lonely in families' (Psalm 68:6) and now I was beginning to assert that I was part of a family.

Things were now different in my married life as well, and not all of that was easy. In our relationship, previously Stuart would say, 'Right, well, I've got some holiday brochures and I'm thinking we'll go here…' and he'd show me all the things he'd researched – because he always chose where we would go for a holiday. He made the choices about everything we did, because he had to. But then one day – I remember it clearly, because it had never happened before – I looked up at him and said, 'But I don't want to go there!' I'd never said anything like that before and Stuart didn't know how to deal with it.

We then actually began to go through quite a difficult phase in our marriage because I was becoming someone he'd not seen before. I was beginning to want to have choices and I was becoming someone different to the person he'd married. Basically, who I really was, was beginning to be seen, and that was hard for us both to work through.

Don't underestimate the impact that coming into freedom from lifelong behaviour patterns can have, for the person themselves and for their surrounding relationships, especially in a marriage. We get used to one another and know one another's strengths and weaknesses. Over time, we begin to instinctively know what the other will like and dislike, even what they might say in a given situation, and we become easy with one another, settling into a pattern of working together. To bring significant change into a relationship like this, even change that is good, will upset the equilibrium and bring uncertainty and confusion into the mix. Stuart couldn't quite get to grips with my wanting to choose for myself now; it seemed undermining to him and it also seemed undermining and controlling to me if he tried to carry on making the choices for me as he had always done. A whole new realm of 'getting to know' one another opened up and it wasn't always easy! So, in the immediate aftermath of those prayer sessions which had formed 'part two' of the deliverance, all these changes were starting to happen.

In addition to all this, I had ongoing physical struggles, and by this time I also wore a neck collar for support. Three times a week I had to go for physiotherapy and heat treatment on my neck. The first half of the physiotherapy was traction, whereby my neck was put in a harness and weights were put on my back in order to stretch out my neck vertebrae. Then after about ten to fifteen minutes I would have 'heat treatment', which would involve a machine that had two 'arms' and some kind of heat ray that would come out between them. I would have to lie flat and very still, and then they would position the 'arms' very carefully, according to wherever they wanted the heat to penetrate. I was also given a bell. If I wanted to move or go to the toilet, I could ring the bell so that the staff would come and switch the machine off for a while.

Generally, I just laid there without any problems; it was only about twenty minutes to half an hour, so I didn't normally find it necessary to ring the bell. I'd been for hundreds of these appointments in the run-up to those two prayer sessions because I'd been three times a week for months. Anyway, I was attending these appointments around the time of having the reoccurring dream about my hair being set on fire. On the first appointment after that final session of prayer, I remember being set up as usual for the heat treatment and, as always, I was lying there half-asleep. But then, all of a sudden, something happened. I started to smell horrendous burning.

Immediately, the dream came into sharp focus and once again I found myself reliving the episode of the bullies hitting me around the head, the incident that I'd dreamed about and which kick-started all the reliving and surfacing of trauma. It was frightening as I once again began to relive that event. But then, quite abruptly, the whole reliving experience came to a halt because a thought cut in across it all. I thought, 'No, that's not where you are now, you have a bell. Ring the bell.' So, I rang the bell and I saw a nurse coming towards me. Then I saw her start running and shouting; she pulled away the trolley with the machine on it literally just in time, just as it went up in flames! What I had been able to smell was actually the machine short-circuiting.

That had never happened in all the many, many times I had been for heat treatment, and the staff said they'd never known that to happen before. But it just so happened to take place the first time I went after having that prayer. Yes, maybe it was a 'coincidence', but I don't believe in those! Maybe it was 'an attack' designed to pull me back, but what the whole experience actually taught me was: 'Those things do not rule in you anymore.' Yes, the event had the power to take me straight back to where I had been before, but instead, somewhere in myself I found that I had the power to switch it off and say, 'No, that's not ruling me anymore. I have a bell.' After that I went back home and quickly got in touch with Ray and told him what had happened. I said, 'I know I'm free because I rang the bell!'

He thought what had happened was pretty significant as well. And so I continued this journey of discovering that I could make all these choices.

The day after that 'burning and bell' episode, something else happened to seal what God had done.

Stuart hadn't said anything to me but on the same day I'd had the burning machine incident, on his way to work, he'd passed a house which had a big notice in the window that said 'Kittens – free to a good home'. He walked past the sign again the day after and couldn't get it out of his mind. So, on the third day, on his way home from work, he went in. Their cat had recently had a litter of eight kittens which were all tortoiseshell except for one which was black and white. Stuart said, 'I'll take that one!' He came home with a cardboard box and said to me: 'I've got something in here that I think is meant for you.' I could hear all this scratching about and there it was, this poor little kitten trying to get out of the box! When I saw it, I just immediately thought of the moment that I'd seen Jesus holding out a black and white kitten! It was amazing.

I then said, 'Oh! I'll have to buy cat food!' and I went straight to the local pet shop to buy a basket and various other things. I'd never gone around a shop and picked things out in that way before, but now, I just went around choosing a basket, and this and that, and a little collar with a bell in the middle of it. I was just picking all these things and making choices without even thinking about it, which was all very new for me!

I wasn't far from where Ray and Jean lived and so I thought, 'I'm going to go and tell them!' So, I went around to their house and Ray opened the door.

'Are you and Jean busy?' I asked.

'Is there something you need?' Ray asked.

'Well, do you want to come and see my kitten?' I said.

They both just looked at me, processing what I'd just said, and then replied, 'Yes! We will come and see your kitten.' So, they came and looked at this tiny furry bundle; exactly the same kind of black and white kitten that I'd 'seen' Jesus holding out to me.

'What are you going to call her?' they asked. 'You could call her "Promise". It would be like the promise of all that God's got for you.' But I didn't like that name. I called her 'Pledge', which is another word for promise. Everyone else thought that it was taken from the name of a brand of furniture polish because the kitten had a shiny coat, and we let them think that. But I knew what it really meant.

This cat turned out to be part of my therapy. I think she missed her mother and so she used to run up the back of my leg, which hurt like mad, and sit on my shoulder. If I took her down, she would just do it again. So, when I was in the house it was like walking around like Long John Silver with the parrot on his shoulder, except I was walking around with a kitten on my shoulder!

I'm not particularly a cat lover or a dog lover, but at that time, having the cat was a reflection of what God was saying to me: 'You are able, you are useful, you can look after things.' The other side of the 'pledge' was that I had pledged with God that I was going to do my best to help other people to be set free, and I felt like He pledged with me to show me that I could look after things and would be able to help people and do many other things in life. That was the significance of the kitten coming into our home.

Chapter Eighteen: Burying the Pseudo Truth

From there I went into a time where I began to give myself to looking out for other people; wanting to help if they were struggling, and wanting to pray for them if they were ill. I began to train in different types of counselling, and in stepping out to pray for the sick. It didn't matter that I was often in pain myself; often I would see people healed then and there. And sometimes I'd share things with people that would encourage them, or build them up, or help them in some other way.

I also felt God start to deepen my understanding about the importance of my baptism in water. It is actually only basic theology, but it was about the fact that when I went under the water, me as the person I was up to that point died with Christ. I was identifying with His death and dying with Him. I went under the water as a person born into sin, with distress and pain, with unforgiveness and anger deep in my being, held in torment by demons. I went into the water as nobody, with no voice, suicidal and preferring nonexistence, traumatised, violated, physically ill and living with the consequences of other's misdeeds. Such was the 'old self' that was me on that day. However, at the moment that I came up out of the water, I was raised up as a new creation in Christ Jesus. Romans 6:4 says: 'We were therefore buried with him through baptism into death in order that, just as Christ was raised from the dead through the glory of the Father, we too may live a new life.' I felt like He was showing me that He had done that for me and I could now live in the fullness of that.

Then it dawned on me that I didn't have to live in anything of what was the 'old self' (Romans 6:6). Those things that had been done to me, taught to me, or said to me. Those things I had been taunted with, tempted by, or had assailed me. In fact, any other thing that had been trying to keep me locked in and distressed, I didn't have to live with any longer. The 'old self' was dead; dead and gone. I was a new creation and no longer had any need to be subjected to anything the 'old self' or the enemy could say to me.

I could choose to live in the fullness of the new creation and of what God was saying to me and of what God was making me to be. He made me to be a new creation in that one moment He died; but He's also making me, in an ongoing sense, to be that new creation. So, I can live in the fullness of that, or I can listen to the 'old self', because the battle in my head was constantly there:

> 'You're nobody!'
> 'But that's not true, I'm a child of God.' (Romans 8:15)
> 'You're useless!'
> 'But God's given me something to do that He prepared for me before the foundation of the world. I'm not useless.' (Jeremiah 1:5)
> 'You don't belong.'
> 'But He's adopted me into His family.' (Ephesians 1:5)

It was a constant war, but now I had the knowledge that I could choose which one I let win, despite it being a battle. Now the power of those demons that had been at work in my life had been broken and it was over to me to choose.

I had become much more aware of the battles that could rage in my own head, and it was as if there was a war between two opposing 'truths'. At any point the 'truth' that I was 'a nobody', 'no good', 'useless' and 'not fit to exist' would rule and caused me to behave according to that 'truth' – after all, these things were true about me, weren't they? But, of course, this was *not* the truth, it was a 'pseudo truth' (also known as a lie). It only *seemed* true because it was based upon what I had always been told – what I'd always known and believed – and most importantly, because it *felt* like the truth. So then my behaviour would be based upon all this pseudo truth which I'd been 'conditioned' to believe for my entire life.

When we are subjected to things like manipulation and control, when we are oppressed and kept down, something crushes our spirit, our inner being, and our response is to act out of how we have been led to see ourselves. We may begin to emotionally retreat, pull back and withdraw, or alternatively we may 'dig our heels in' and become defensive and stubborn in our interactions. We may also begin to isolate ourselves from those who seem to be 'right' or 'successful' in what they are doing, thinking, 'I could never be like that.' We can put up an inner guard against people or situations as a way of defending ourselves from further hurt because we assume history will repeat itself. We are no longer clear and honest with other people as we keep part of ourselves back, retreating into our own little bubble. All of this is the work of an enemy to keep us oppressed and subjected to unwritten, unbiblical laws of how we must live and behave.

In addition to this, we can also assume that we will not be heard, so we either do not bother to speak or act, or alternatively, we become defensive and overactive in speaking and acting, in order to make sure that we *have* been heard. We can inwardly take everything people say and filter it through an inner prism of suspicion, mistrust and guardedness. We even learn to mistrust the 'nudges' of the Holy Spirit and think, 'Maybe it's just me.' So, we hold back in contributing into the corporate meetings because we think we have nothing of value to say.

Eventually, we learn that we should not trust in our own judgement and so mistrust even ourselves and our own motives. Over time, we lose the ability to make a clear choice or decision and consider ourselves inadequate and weak in our faith. This was my behaviour according to the pseudo truth which I had firmly believed. But, of course, the pseudo truth is nothing but a bunch of lies that the enemy will keep us feeding on because he wants us to remain a victim. But actually, in our walk with God we are victorious because we are hidden in the One who is *the* victor (Colossians 3:3).

Until this point I had believed the lies because they had always been there and they *felt* true, they *felt* like reality and were all I had ever known. Until the point of 'part two' of the deliverance, the pseudo truth ruled and consequently my behaviour was ruled by it. So, if I found anything to be too threatening I would simply withdraw from the situation. If I couldn't physically withdraw, then it was as if something kicked in that caused a complete dissociation, so I'd be present in the body, but somewhere inside I would have completely switched off into a much safer place (or so it seemed). I didn't consciously choose to be like that but it was a learned behaviour, a defence mechanism that had always been there over the years. I didn't 'feel' any sense of good, happy or positive things as it was too risky to hope to ever feel anything like that; rather, I lived in the place of always expecting a backlash, with a creeping foreboding about everything I said or didn't say, did or didn't do, constantly living 'on eggshells', as the saying goes, and I couldn't escape.

But now I had begun to recognise what had happened when I rose out of the baptism pool. Now I was a 'new creation' (2 Corinthians 5:17) and I realised there was another, better truth, a truth that was the 'real truth' and the truth that sets us free (John 8:36).

Every thought I had, I had to take hold of and make it obedient to God's truth, and in doing that I knew that God was demolishing some internal personal strongholds (2 Corinthians 10:5). Every time I was struggling with *Nemo* I sensed God was helping me, reminding me of the 'real truth'. I would think about coming up from my baptism choking and hanging onto the minister's robes, but I would reassure myself that when I did come up, I came up to new life, and so I was a new creation in Christ Jesus. He has given me 'a future and a hope' (Jeremiah 29:11, ESV), He has given me a purpose; there are plans that He has for me, and the old me has been dead and buried for good.

2 Corinthians 5:17 tells us, 'Therefore, if anyone is in Christ, he is a new creation. The old has passed away; behold, the new has come' (ESV). As Christians, we don't need to carry the baggage of our past into our future; rather, the baggage is taken from us, gone, passed away, left at the bottom of the baptismal pool, and our future holds newness.

This battle in the head between the pseudo truth and the real truth is what has to happen after we have experienced any deliverance ministry; now we have to learn to walk free in every moment of every day. Scripture says that 'we have the mind of Christ' (1 Corinthians 2:16). We, the Church, are to be a people walking in the fact that we are and are becoming a new creation. Sadly, so many people are in a place like I was; continuing to walk in the darkness of the 'old self' instead of walking in the light of being and becoming new. For me, *Nemo* was a self-fulfilling curse which needed to be repented of and broken with the help of deliverance prayer, but equally importantly, it needed to be overturned day by day with the real truth, and there's a whole process in walking free and remaining free. It therefore isn't enough to have prayers of deliverance, to respond to a prophetic word or a sermon in a single moment in time and expect for that alone to free us from all our struggles to overcome. The individual 'setting free' moments are, of course, vitally important, but then we have to live out those moments in our ongoing, everyday lives. This is what I call 'walking free'.

After the first two 'parts' of my deliverance and the revelation that I'd had about the importance of that moment of my baptism, I began to realise that I didn't get into a state of volcanic eruption in quite the same way anymore. Oh, I would get uptight and frustrated, but then I would realise that was because I needed to talk, I needed to say something. But I'd never seen that modelled before. I'd never realised that the reason that I was blowing up was because everything had always been bottled up deep within me somewhere. When I was with

Stuart and other people it was as if deep down a voice was saying, 'You don't really know me. You don't know what I like and don't like, you don't know what I've had to live through' – though I never consciously thought like that – and now I needed to learn how to communicate.

Even today, if Stuart and I have a disagreement, I need to stop and recognise that I need to say things like, 'Look, I'm sorry, but I'm getting worked up here and feeling emotional because I really can't face doing that. What do you think?' Stuart has learned to say things such as, 'I'd like to do this. What do you think?' and I'll respond back.

We learned to work out our disagreements in a better way because I had realised that I needed to sit down and *talk*, to say exactly what it was that I was feeling. Therefore, whereas previously I'd communicated in monosyllables or very short sentences such as 'Beans!' or 'Park Drive!', a new level of communication had now begun in my life. And other people started to notice the difference.

We had friends in the church because they had been Stuart's friends and by default they became my friends. I hadn't personally interacted with them much before, but now I began engaging with them in conversation; I actually started communicating with them. There was one couple that had four children and I would sometimes go to their house and help around the place with a bit of cleaning, or maybe I'd babysit. I might stay on for a meal, or Stuart would come and we'd have a meal together with them, and then Stuart and I would babysit so that they could have some time out together. I was often there when the lady was preparing a meal, and I would sit and watch her. I'd ask, 'How do you make that? Can you show me how to make that?' So, from this dear lady I learned over time how to make all manner of basic things, such as apple crumble, chilli and different types of casserole. I'd just ask her and she'd show me what to do.

God used this couple in their loving of others, in the church and in my life, and this is so important in a person's healing. Jean, Ray's wife, had three children and liked to sew, and sometimes I would babysit for them as well. Back then it was cheaper to make your own clothes than to buy them from the shops, so I would ask Jean, 'How can I make a dress?' She taught me how to sew, to make my own clothes, make a pair of curtains and other things for the home. I learned over time how to be the wife that I wanted to be, how to look after Stuart and myself in the basics of life, and how to make things for our home. So, I learned from other people around me in the church, just as you would learn from one another in a family.

Their input into me as another family member alongside them was so important; it built into me something of the belonging to a family which I had never had. Oh, I was good at the serving bit; I never needed to learn that. I had served in many ways, usually in a hidden way, like cleaning the toilets midweek, cleaning in the building, or doing the washing up after church events. I would do all those things that no one would really notice because, after all, that was where I belonged, wasn't it? Good Christian values were helping to hide a real need at that point.

Take a look at those in your church who serve regularly 'behind the scenes'; many are called to those things and there is no issue with it at all. But some will be serving in such a manner because they can hide behind a teacloth or a mop and bucket. Romans 12:3-8 teaches us that in whatever we do – whether that is to clean the toilets, speak from the platform, make the tea, or prophesy – we do those things to serve one another. None of us should 'think of [ourselves] more highly than [we] ought, but rather think of [ourselves]with sober judgment' (v. 3). We shouldn't feel we have to hide ourselves behind what we do, either. We can all serve in many different ways, so let's encourage every member to be free to do many things and allow their voice to be heard too.

Now I was having to learn, learn from others, to receive from others, to be a part with others and to begin to trust that the prophetic word was not just a disjointed thing, a speaking of words and then moving on and waiting for the kickback. I was realising that the prophetic word is for family; to encourage them, to strengthen them, to comfort them and equally to serve them as much as cleaning the toilets served them. I was learning to come out from behind the teacloth.

As a child, when I had gone for appointments at the Child Guidance Clinic, sometimes the staff would ask me to draw pictures of how I saw myself in the family unit. I always drew the same pictures right through into adulthood. I drew stick figures of Mother, Father and my brother and sister watching the television and then over on the other side of the sheet of paper I drew a stick figure doing the ironing. Or other similar pictures such as on holiday where I was carrying everything whilst the others had an ice cream. And that was me. I very much saw myself as not being part of the family unit; I was outside of it, nonexistent, *Nemo*. Somehow deep in the subconscious I believed that the only reason that I did exist was to make the chores happen; I was outside of the family rather than part of it. So, being in church and being drawn in as part of the family was the church saying to me, 'We include you.' I had real battles in allowing myself to be part of that.

I strongly believe that the Church not only has the key message of hope, but it is also part of the healing process. It is where we learn to accept one another, look out for one another, even at times challenge and confront one another but then forgive one another, fight for one another, pray for one another and love one another. Together we are the people of God and by our love for one another the world will see that we are His followers (John 13:35). 'Beloved, if God so loved us, we also ought to love one another' (1 John 4:11, ESV).

Chapter Nineteen: Broken Strongholds

Soon after the two 'knockout' prayer sessions, Mother's sister, my aunt, rang me up. At this particular time my grandmother was living with her because she now needed quite a lot of help and support, and could no longer really look after herself. According to their doctor, my grandmother was suffering from the onset of Alzheimer's disease and was frequently having hallucinations. But my aunty argued against this: 'She isn't having hallucinations. She knows exactly what she is saying. The thing is that she is telling me what's going to happen; she's telling me the future. She tells me "this and this and this" is going to happen and it does, always the day afterwards.'

Now, my aunt was not a churchgoer. She didn't believe in God or anything else, and was the most down-to-earth person in the whole family. But she said to us, 'I don't know what to do because the doctors keep saying that it's hallucinations, but how can it be hallucinations when she's telling me what's going to happen tomorrow?'

For instance, my grandmother would sit in the corner in her chair and then she would suddenly say, 'The floor, the floor, mop it all up, mop it all up, there's water everywhere, the washing machine's leaking, there's water everywhere, there's water everywhere!' yet there'd be nothing amiss. But then the next day the washing machine would leak and there'd be water everywhere. Or she'd say, 'Oh, be careful of that man that's knocking on everybody's door because he's a robber and he's going to rob the people on the street.' But there'd be nobody knocking on the door and there'd be nobody to be seen. But the following day it turned out that somebody had knocked on the door and when my aunt answered it, they said that they'd got the wrong house and then carried on knocking on the doors down the street. So, my aunt watched him because she thought that that was a bit strange. Then later on in the week they discovered that people had been burgled that day.

This kind of thing was happening nearly every day – my grandmother was speaking about things the day before they happened. So, my aunt said that this couldn't be hallucinations and she thought the only person she knew who might be able to help was her niece because she went to church, meaning me! My aunt asked me, 'Will you come over and talk to your grandmother, because I don't like this, it's frightening me?' I told her that I'd ring her back.

As I put the phone down, I thought, 'This is strange.' This was taking place only a few weeks after the man in the south of England had asked me about the occult in my family, which I had denied as I hadn't known of anything. However, now my aunt was describing this situation and I didn't know what to think, or what to do, either! I decided to phone Ray.

I said to him, 'I told the man who prayed for me that there was no occult in my family so he didn't pray about that, but this sounds weird.'

Ray agreed. 'This seems a bit suspect. It sounds to me like something you ought to be careful about.'

Strangely, at the moment that Ray was on the phone with me, my mother made one of her surprise visits, which she was in the habit of doing at that time; she just turned up at the door.

She could see I was on the phone, so she sat down. Ray was going to ring off, but I had this feeling that it was 'meant to be'. Stuart was at work, so I said, 'Mother has arrived and I'm going to ask her about this thing with my grandmother. I'd like you to be here if you can.' If there was going to be anything else to tackle, or any other difficulty, I wanted someone with me!

Ray and his wife came over. We sat at the kitchen table and I asked my mother if there was anything to do with the occult in her family, and she just replied, 'Oh, no, no, not at all!'

I elaborated, 'Well, Aunty has just rung and she's told me all these things about Grandmother.' But Mother pretended she knew nothing.

Then a startling thing happened in front of everyone. I began to have an open vision – as I mentioned before, this is where something superimposes itself over what you're actually looking at. I was looking at the kitchen wall behind where Mother was sitting and I saw the wall of another room. On the wall of the other room was a picture of a Red Indian chief with his headdress on, with lots of amazingly colourful feathers in it. I said, 'I'm seeing something right now.' I started describing this picture and the room I was seeing.

'Stop, stop, stop!' Mother insisted, and started screaming. And then the truth finally came out.

Apparently, in their younger days her mother and father, my grandparents, had both been heavily involved in the occult. Grandfather had served in the Far East in the war and so he had become interested, and then involved in, voodoo, black magic, tarot card reading, palm reading and reading tea leaves. He had become a master in some of these Eastern 'traditions' and after that continued to stay heavily involved in all manner of occult practices. And my grandmother had been a highly regarded clairvoyant medium in the spiritualist church! Not only that, but when Mother was born, because she was the firstborn, they had decided that she should carry on the line of 'the gifts' from them.

My grandparents therefore tried to pray for Mother and school her into the things of the occult, but it frightened her too much and she didn't fully want it. She was, what they called 'a difficult child', so they gave up on her. Their second daughter, my aunt, wasn't a firstborn so they never tried to encourage her in these things. But as a result, Mother had a lifelong obsession with horoscopes and all manner of superstitious sayings, and believed in 'second sight', although she herself never seemed to operate in that, as far as I knew.

As we sat at the table, my mother said that I was describing the room that my grandmother was now living in at my aunt's house. I hadn't been there since I was a child, so I hadn't seen this room as it now was. She said that the picture on the wall that I was describing was the Red Indian chief that was my grandmother's spirit guide.

Then Mother said, 'They didn't get very far with me, so when you were born, you were the firstborn and they wanted you to carry on 'the gifts' instead of me, but I wouldn't let them'. Yikes! I had no idea.

Ray sat there listening to all of this and was probably having a complete panic, because it was still the early days of the church coming into the things of the Spirit; we were breaking through into using the spiritual gifts in church life, and I had been moving in the prophetic, words of knowledge (1 Corinthians 12:8) and so on.

The question was then, 'Does this mean that what you have been bringing is the real thing, or is it all coming from the wrong source?'

I said, 'Well, I have had no sense of anything to do with the occult, and the voice that I hear has always been the Man in the Picture, His voice, which I have always believed to be Jesus.'

Ray didn't quite know what to do, so he decided to ring the man he'd sent me to see in the south of England, because he had first mentioned the occult.

Today I would recognise that the enemy does not uncover his own work, it is the light of truth that uncovers the darkness. Jesus was once accused of casting out demons by the ruler of demons, and His answer was: 'If Satan drives out Satan, he is divided against himself. How then can his kingdom stand?' (Matthew 12:24-26). No, when darkness is exposed it is because the light, the true light that is Jesus, has come to expose and deal with that darkness.

But back then we needed to be sure. Ray explained to the man everything that had just been revealed, and the man advised that I shouldn't go to see my grandmother unless she was willing to repent. If Grandmother was willing to repent then I could go, share the gospel with her and pray for her, but if not, I should have nothing more to do with her, and renounce anything to do with her as well as renounce the occult, which I was told I needed to do anyway to ensure that I didn't go on to unwittingly bring anything from a 'wrong source'.

I rang my aunt and said that I was willing to come and talk to Grandmother if she was willing to put everything to do with clairvoyance behind her, and repent; turn away from it, and have nothing more to do with it. If she was willing to do this then I was willing to come and pray with her to ask God to set her free and to lift any oppression and fear from her which had been caused by all this.

My aunt had never been involved in anything herself but had remembered her parents going off to the spiritualist church and she told me about it all, including others in the family using a Ouija board in that same room that my grandmother was now living in. She said she didn't want, and had never wanted, anything to do with it all and agreed to speak to Grandmother.

My aunt later got back to me to say, 'Your grandmother doesn't think she's got anything to be sorry or repent about, she doesn't think she's got anything to turn away from, nor does she think it's wrong. She's going to continue to use her spirit guide and she does not want to do anything that you suggested.' I simply replied, 'Well, I'm not going to come, then!'

We met up with Ray yet again so that I could renounce everything to do with the occult, and then he was able to pray with me.

I sat at our dining table and I prayed. I thanked God for bringing all of this into the light and then I said that I didn't want any part of any of it. I said I didn't want any of these things in my life and I named all the things that had come out; every single one of a big, long list of occult-related things, from tea leaves and horoscopes to black magic and voodoo, and everything in-between. I said that I did not want to bear any gifts that did not come from God and I renounced every single thing by name.

The next day I received a phone call from my aunt. My grandmother had died, passing away at exactly the same time that I was renouncing anything further to do with her and all the occult things that she and my grandfather had tried to pass on to me without my knowledge. My feeling is that God gave her this last opportunity to turn away from all of this dark stuff and to get right with Him, but she refused it.

From that point in time I knew I was free from all kinds of occult things in my family line that previously I had not even been aware of.

It therefore turned out that the man who had spoken to me about the occult in the first instance had been totally right. At the time I had thought he had got it completely wrong because I had no knowledge of it.

Reflecting back on the time as a schoolgirl doing the project on stories of local hauntings, I was getting interested in the paranormal. When I woke up in the middle of the night hearing the words 'No more' I now believe that to have been the voice of God. I believe that was God stopping me from going any further down that wrong road. How good He is!

I had also said 'no' to the man in answer to his question about whether my mother had another child before I was born. He seemed to think that I was carrying something from Mother because of this lost child, but I had just insisted that that wasn't the case. Well, I found out, many years later, after my mother had died, that he had also been correct about that. I found a diary of my mother's and letters to my father that detailed how she was pregnant. It was not long after they had been married, well before I had been conceived. I was born two years after my parents' marriage but this letter was dated the very same year as their marriage. I then found another letter from a friend of hers detailing her condolences: 'I'm so very sorry to hear about the loss of your baby, very sad news.' So, it was evident that she had indeed had a pregnancy resulting in loss before I came along. After that, I felt as if everything that the man said that I needed to be released from, even the things that I was unaware of at that time, I had indeed been released from.

Release had come, and everything in me that spoke of not belonging, of being nobody without a voice, could now be overcome. That which spoke of having no identity, being of no use, needing to keep quiet and disappear – to all of this I now had the power to say, 'No, that's a lie!' However, even today it is still possible to fall prey to the taunting voice that says things like, 'You shouldn't be here, you don't belong.'

The enemy will always try to pull us back into the old, dark places. He uses those old lies that we are used to; that old, dark place we may not really want, yet we think of as a 'safe place' because we have never known anything else – just like I thought of the dark coal shed as a safe place because seemingly nothing else could harm me in there. But it wasn't a safe place; there was no light, I couldn't see clearly, it was next to a main road with heavy traffic just outside; it was actually a very unsafe place to be.

Coming out into the light can seem scary and strange after being in such a place for a long time. What is life like on the outside, in the light? What will happen to me in the light? What if I can't cope in the light? To be freed from all the old battles of the mind can sometimes feel a very frightening proposition to contemplate: 'What will I be like without these lies?' But when God is at work to set us free, then we will be held by His everlasting arms.

> The eternal God is a dwelling place, [the safe place]
> And underneath are the everlasting arms;
> And He drove out the enemy before you,
> And said, 'Destroy!'
> (Deuteronomy 33:27, NASB)

Dark places are not safe and the negative, taunting words we battle with in our minds will always be lies which have to be constantly refuted by using the truth to combat them. Those kinds of lies are overpowered by speaking truth to say something like, 'No, I'm here because I've been asked to be here, God has put me here, He has a reason, he wants me here.'

So, God had done all of this deliverance, but what had that actually done? The strongholds in my life were now broken, but that simply meant that now the power rested with me to begin to think and behave differently. I now had to learn how day, by day, by day, to walk in the Spirit; to walk in the light of the truth and not in the darkness of lies. Galatians 5:25 says, 'If we live by the Spirit, let us also walk by the Spirit' (ESV).

The Spirit gives us the enabling as we follow Him. I therefore needed to learn how to listen to the truth because it is the truth that sets us free (John 8:32) and this freedom happens as we increasingly take the truth on board and as we increasingly resist the things of darkness and as we increasingly walk in the way of the truth and not in the 'empty way of life handed down to you from your ancestors' (1 Peter 1:18). Therefore, we don't just get 'set free' in a single moment of deliverance prayer, we have to continually carry on in *every* moment to 'walk free'.

John 8:36 says, 'if the Son sets you free, you will be free indeed'. Some aspects of freedom, revelation and change can take place in a single moment, they are instantaneous, but many things take place over time as we bring our thinking and our mindset in line with the truth. In it all, God is the restorer, the redeemer of all that has been destroyed, eaten away and crushed, over all of our past years. It is the Lord who transforms everything; not just in our spiritual life, but our emotional life, our mental well-being, and even in our physical well-being too; the 'great exchange'.

When a person signs a contract committing to buy a house, in that moment the house becomes legally theirs. However, when they then move in, over the following weeks, months and years, they slowly make that house their home. Similarly, we are legally 'set free' in a single moment when we came to Christ, but then we need to come to a place where we walk free of all that has entangled us previously. Therefore, overpowering *Nemo*, whatever *Nemo* is for you, doesn't take place in a one-off single moment. It is a lifelong walk of rejecting it. And it is in a lifelong walk of rejecting it that we see it being overpowered again and again. That's what it means to walk free.

Whatever your battleground is, the things that you struggle with, whatever your weak areas and difficulties are, the enemy knows about them; he knew all about you before you became a Christian; then, you were living under his dominion, but now you have moved into the light (Colossians 1:13). When you became a Christian, you became a 'new creation' (2 Corinthians 5:17); the enemy no longer rules in your life, and it is maybe important here to say that the enemy doesn't know your every thought. Satan is not the Creator, he is a created being; he is not omniscient, he is not omnipresent; so this clearly teaches us that his powers are limited. It is God who is the all-knowing One, God alone knows our every thought and the state of our hearts. God knows us in our innermost being as He was the One who formed us and knitted us together in the first place (Psalm 139:13).

However, that doesn't mean that all the past stuff of the 'old self' (Romans 6:6) necessarily immediately drops away. Maybe some things do, but some of the key things can remain a battleground, and we will have to battle with them in an ongoing way, and continue to resist them in an ongoing way. We have become a new creation and we are becoming a new creation; it happens in an instant and it takes place over time in an ongoing way as a process throughout our lives.

We need to learn to 'walk in the light' (Isaiah 2:5) and not walk according to darkness. Scripture tells us that we have been changed and we are being changed 'from one degree of glory to another' (2 Corinthians 3:18, ESV) and so I therefore had to begin a lifelong walk of overpowering *Nemo* and learning to live not in nonentity but in the light of identity in Christ. Romans 12:2 says:

> Do not conform to the pattern of this world, but be transformed by the renewing of your mind. Then you will be able to test and approve what God's will is – his good, pleasing and perfect will.

Being transformed is not about us trying to change ourselves. This is not about trying to boost our self-worth and our self-esteem. We're not trying to 'brainwash' ourselves into 'believing the Word' (i.e. I'm not chanting Scripture three times a day as if that in itself will change me). This is about being in relationship with God, through Jesus, following Him, looking at Him, the One who has gone before, the only One who is worthy, and seeing Him as the One who transforms us by the power of His Word at work in us as we walk with Him.

God is the One who takes away from us all the effects of being under the enemy's dominion and brings us into all the benefits of being in His kingdom under His authority. We need to give ourselves to Him and not allow our thinking and behaviour to be moulded by our old way of life, but instead allow our minds to be renewed by the truth of His Word. Our part is to 'not conform', to turn away from the old patterns of our old ways of thinking, and as we do that, as we treasure Him, then He does the transforming. This is how we become the new creation person we are meant to be.

This is subtly different from modern counselling methods; it is God's supernatural work within us. Today there are many highly trained counsellors and therapists using excellent approaches which help to highlight root issues and help to enable changed ways of thinking. We must value people who work in these fields and see them as a very real part of the helping community, alongside those who attend to our physical health. God has many ways of bringing healing, but it is *He* who does the healing, the mending and the freeing. It is God who transforms us; we cannot set ourselves free, we cannot heal ourselves, we cannot change our own thinking patterns, or change ourselves in our own strength. But praise God, He can set us free, He can heal us and does change us as we allow His truth, the 'real truth', to work itself out within us.

Luke 11:24-26 in the ESV says:

> When the unclean spirit has gone out of a person, it passes through waterless places seeking rest, and finding none it says, 'I will return to my house from which I came.' And when it comes, it finds the house swept and put in order. Then it goes and brings seven other spirits more evil than itself, and they enter and dwell there. And the last state of that person is worse than the first.

I am aware that it could be really easy for me to walk back into a place of bondage any day, but I do not want to do that; I want to walk in the truth: 'you will know the truth, and the truth will set you free' (John 8:32). I need to keep on being filled with the Holy Spirit, to keep drinking His Word, to keep communing with Him, praising Him and being, at times, lost in worship of Him.

It is God who will empower me by that truth, by His Word, to daily walk in His truth, to daily walk free. The Bible contains His Word, also He personally is 'the Word' who is working in us and setting us free. He reveals to us the things that we're listening to that are not from Him. As we walk with Him, He reveals those things to us. He will whisper into our thoughts things like, 'But that's a lie; why are you listening to that?' But most of us don't listen to those whispers enough, nor take hold of what they are saying to us. Many people walk around never really realising that they're living part of their lives based on lies that they're listening to all the time. We overcome the enemy 'by the blood of the Lamb and by the word of [our] testimony'

(Revelation 12:11) – that is, the words on our lips. We must learn to say to ourselves 'I will not listen to that' or 'The Bible says', 'the Word says', 'God says', 'It is written…' We must learn to speak the truth back to the lie, and in doing so we overpower it.

Chapter Twenty: According to His Purpose

Today *Nemo* is no longer something that has a strong hold on my life, though it will still try to gain an entry from time to time! But I now have the power to overcome it, I can choose. But because it is so subtle in the way it will try to grab me and take over once more, sometimes things will still happen. Then I realise again, 'I'm listening to a lie here, it's *Nemo* again.' Then I have to make the decision that I'm not going to listen to that lie. I speak truth back to the lie and then I can get back into the truth and get on with life again. It doesn't matter how I feel when the lie comes; I'm usually feeling upset, sad, depressed or bad in some way, but I do not wait for the feeling to pass to tell the enemy I am not listening. However bad I feel, I turn to the truth, the truth sets me free and as the truth settles back within me, the negativity of how I feel begins to lift.

I believe that many people in the Church often believe lies, lies about being unable, not being wanted, being inadequate in some way. How many times have you felt that God has put a psalm, a song, or a prophetic thought in your being, and you say 'That's just me' or don't share such a thing because 'I could never do that'? Or when something is shared that seems tailored by God for you, how many times have you thought, 'This is not meant for me'? If, for example, someone preaches about God's power to heal and then invites people to come forward for prayer, how many times do you actually think, 'Yes! This is for me. I can go forward!'? Actually, I believe most of the time people will think, 'Well, that's fantastic, but I'm not sure that was meant for me!' not because they don't want it, but because they don't see themselves as being in a place where they're able to avail themselves and receive good things like this from the Father.

We somehow subliminally think that all this stuff happens only for other people because we see our own unworthiness, our unrighteousness, and we forget the fact that we were never worthy to receive anything in the first place! But, through Jesus, we have had our sin and unworthiness washed away. In place of that we have received righteousness from God. Read the glories of Romans 3.

In our choices we set our own ceiling; we can choose life, freedom and the real truth, or we can choose the lies of the enemy and the pseudo truth of our own feelings. Do we decide or choose on the basis of how we feel, what we can see or work out for ourselves in our own lives, or do we constantly punch through and see the ceiling raised? Do we choose on the basis of what God has said in His Word? We can set a ceiling on how much we will see the miraculous at work in our lives and in our ministries, or we can raise that ceiling to begin to see far more. Who do we trust to release us from the darkness that has been in our lives; do we put our trust in ourselves, in others, or in God?

We all need to learn to speak the truth to ourselves. Therefore, I should no longer call myself *Nemo*, or nobody, or no man, but nor am I to tell myself 'I am somebody'. This is not about myself, but rather I am to look to Him and remind myself of His Word which says, 'God deliberately chose ... "nobodies" to expose the hollow pretensions of the "somebodies"' (1 Corinthians 1:27, *MSG*) and I praise Him that He does this. The antidote to feeling like a nobody is not to seek to be a 'somebody', but to focus on Him who chooses nobodies to destroy what the somebodies consider important. I do not seek to be a 'somebody', but I seek to live my life in relationship with Him knowing that I am hidden in the One who Himself is the Somebody! John 18:37 says, 'Everyone who is of the truth hears My voice' (NASB) and John 10:27 says, 'My sheep hear my voice' (ESV).

So whilst we certainly can encounter deliverance in many and different ways, and whilst demons can be told to go in a single time of prayer, true freedom will come from living daily in the truth. Truth is in our relationship with God and has to be walked in constantly.

So, in my being delivered and set free in an instant from the spirit of rejection, there has been an ongoing walk with Him of hearing His voice. At times it was a real battle to choose to believe His truth that declares to me that I am part of His body, chosen and called by Him; however, these days I no longer need Him to remind me of this particular truth on a daily basis as it has become living and real within me. I now know I *do* belong.

The antidote to feeling useless is not to continually listen to the enemy accusing me of being useless, nor to tell myself that I am useful, but to remind myself and the enemy that God has called me for His purpose. Romans 8:28 says, 'we know that in all things God works for the good of those who love him, who have been called according to his purpose' – therefore, neither you nor I are useless.

Walking free is therefore largely about taking our thoughts captive; we get hold of these thoughts, brought to us out of our 'old self', the experiences of the past, or the accusations of others, and we refute them with the truth of God's Word. 2 Corinthians 10:3-5 says:

> For though we live in the world, we do not wage war as the world does. The weapons we fight with are not the weapons of the world. On the contrary, they have divine power to demolish strongholds. We demolish arguments and every pretension that sets itself up against the knowledge of God, and we take captive every thought to make it obedient to Christ.

In context this scripture has a much wider application, but it speaks to us personally, too, exhorting us to pull down wrong ways of thinking, pull down everything in us that would work against God's purposes for our lives. As we challenge and speak back to the things that have held us, so, brick by brick, we demolish the strongholds, and as a result the walls that have surrounded us come down. It is not in our own strength but through relationship with Him and the work of the Spirit in us; it is His divine power that works in us (Ephesians 3:20).

The 'weapons of our warfare' include daily walking with Him, spending time in His Word, getting to know it and letting the power of it affect our lives. It includes prayer and learning to go to Him with our cares and difficulties as well as to honour and praise Him, learning to depend on Him for our needs and keeping on being filled with the Spirit (Ephesians 5:18). These things are all part of our armoury, and the warfare we are in involves training our minds to daily overcome the 'old self' and live as the new person in Christ that we are, putting off the old and putting on the new (Ephesians 4:22-24).

This is what is pictured in our baptism. Have you ever wondered why we only baptise a person in water once and not frequently, as we do with celebrating the Lord's supper? Well, we celebrate the Lord's Supper, communion, breaking of bread, because as they had supper together Jesus took the bread and broke it and said to His disciples 'do this in remembrance of me' (Luke 22:19). We need to constantly remind ourselves of Jesus; who He is and what He has done. And we do it together; we are drawn into community together, remembering Him together, encouraging one another together until He comes again (1 Corinthians 11:26). We need to celebrate the Lord's Supper frequently.

But baptism is picturing something that happened once, in a moment of time, a point in history that changed the world. It is a one-time event; Jesus died and rose again. And so it is for us; a one-time event whereby the 'old self' that we once were died with Christ, and now we have been made new as we were raised with Him. At the core of our being we are a new creation in Christ. His Spirit will help us in outworking all the potential of that new self as we walk with Him.

Ephesians 4:22-24 says:

> You were taught, with regard to your former way of life, to put off your old self, which is being corrupted by its deceitful

> desires; to be made new in the attitude of your minds; and to put on the new self, created to be like God in true righteousness and holiness.

It is always a time to put on the new self!

Once we profess with our lips our belief and faith in Christ and who He is and what He has done, it is hugely important to be baptised as a way of publicly declaring this. It is very important because we are not only declaring our faith to those around us but we are declaring to the principalities and powers in 'heavenly realms' that now we are a new creation in Him (Ephesians 6:12). And, this act of baptism becomes from there on in, a point of reference in our battle with the enemy. I can now say to the enemy every time He assaults me, 'Be gone. I am no longer that person. I am now a new creation in Christ and I am now free to follow Him.'

We are a people born of the Spirit and we are now in the age of the Spirit, so let's live our lives in the power of the Spirit. We need to push through to hide in Him in times of difficulty, pushing through for miracles and pushing through to stand in Him even in times of seeming success. We need to learn to make right choices even when no one else but God can see us making that choice. This is what most of what is known as 'spiritual warfare' is all about. It's not just about praying for others, other situations and so on, it is also about the warfare that goes on within our own being; our own thinking and our own head. Ephesians 6 details how we have been given everything we need to resist the powers of darkness that assail us, exhorting us to 'stand firm' in what we know is true (v. 6).

Over the years, as I've learned to resist the enemy like this. In all the difficult times I speak in tongues and I go back to those scriptures that build into me perseverance and faith. One of my favourite scriptures is from Habakkuk 3:17-19:

Though the fig-tree does not bud
and there are no grapes on the vines,
though the olive crop fails
and the fields produce no food,
though there are no sheep in the sheepfold
and no cattle in the stalls,
yet I will rejoice in the LORD,
I will be joyful in God my Saviour.
The Sovereign LORD is my strength;
he makes my feet like the feet of a deer,
he enables me to tread on the heights.

I read scriptures like this over and over until that moment when it becomes real within me and I can arise from that time knowing that whatever happens, I am kept by His power and I can exult in the Lord again as He once more becomes my strength. We constantly have to overcome the enemy, who will keep trying to resurrect the 'old self' within us and rob us of our hope and our voice.

We are reborn into freedom and not intended to be slaves to the 'old self', the old lies, the old ways that our family history has dictated to us. They are no more: 'It is for freedom that Christ has set us free. Stand firm, then, and do not let yourselves be burdened again by a yoke of slavery' (Galatians 5:1).

As I entered into a season of getting on with life, I still had an ongoing battle to combat all the lies that I was still hearing. I didn't realise that so much of what I had been listening to was lies, and I didn't realise to what degree I had been shaped by those lies until I started combating them. When I reached a point where I thought I was getting there, then God would unveil a whole different set of lies that I'd been listening to. Previously, I didn't seem to have the power to fight the battle, and that was because it had a strong hold on me and that's why it needed somebody to pray and break its power. But now, even though I was still battling with lies, somehow the power base had shifted to me; somehow I could withstand the lies. And so began the reshaping into something new.

God had said to me that He would bring about a 'great exchange' and His Word declares Him to be all-powerful in so many ways, including in setting people free. 'Nothing [is] impossible with God' (Luke 1:37, ESV). The power of God is at work today to set the captives free (Luke 4:18). God wants to liberate us. He does perform a 'great exchange' by the power of the Spirit; He does give freedom instead of captivity, light instead of darkness, comfort instead of mourning, beauty instead of ashes, joy instead of despair (Isaiah 61:1-3).

When we come to Him we are set free from the authority that Satan has had over our lives and we are brought into God's great kingdom under His supreme authority. Colossians 1:13 says, 'For he has rescued us from the dominion of darkness and brought us into the kingdom of the Son he loves' – we have shifted to a higher authority. We can live more and more in this freedom, this kingdom we have come into, instead of being trapped in darkness, tormented by sin and fear.

Isaiah 61:7 says:

> Instead of your shame you will receive a double portion, and instead of disgrace you will rejoice in your inheritance. And so you will inherit a double portion in your land …

There is an exchange 'out of' for an 'in to'. It's not just a learning to 'cope with life', nor is it a 'coming to terms' with things, not even a 'learning to manage one's emotions'. That is how the non-Christian gets through, by trying to free themselves, change themselves and manage themselves. As I mentioned earlier, I often say to people that I could never have 'come to terms' with child abuse, it should never happen to anyone, but before the deliverance that's what I was trying to do – I was trying to 'learn to cope with life', I was trying to 'manage my emotions' and trying to 'come to terms with' the horror of what had gone on, but I just couldn't do that.

So many of us try to 'come to terms with' things that have happened to us; we attempt to manage our emotions, especially when the enemy tries hard to stir them up. We do not need to try, though; God has already broken the power of those things that affect us so much, because we died with Him and are raised a new creation in Him, the old has gone and 'the new has come' (2 Corinthians 5:17, ESV) – this is the real truth! With God, there is an end to the old broken 'me' and the birthing of a new 'me'. There is a planting and rooting into Him, that is what is transforming; we are taken into His purposes and He is about transforming communities, impacting nations and building His Church. We can be part of that; having put off the old, we put on the new and we are transformed to show forth His glory and power.

We have been redeemed from the 'empty way of life handed down ... from [our] ancestors' (1 Peter 1:18), and those empty ways no longer hold us. There is no need to be blighted by the past, isolated by it into our own bubble where we protect ourselves from further hurt by putting a wall up to others. Rather, it is about allowing God to help us dismantle the wall and move into community. Isolation is a huge ploy of the enemy. He can work on us to get us to isolate ourselves, whereby he can then further speak lies and accusations to us and we isolate ourselves even more and become trapped in a downward spiral.

We need to trust that not only do we walk with a God of the impossible, but that He will fulfil His Word. It doesn't mean that we will have an easy life, and not every prayer will be answered as we would like, but we can trust in Him and we can trust that He is with us. He knows our weaknesses, as Hebrews 4:15 tells us:

> For we do not have a high priest who is unable to feel sympathy for our weaknesses, but we have one who has been tempted in every way, just as we are – yet he did not sin.

God will help us in all that comes our way. He will help us by giving us His grace and strength to handle our emotions, to push past the temptation to believe all the old lies, and He will, through the power of His Spirit, change us as we take hold of the truth.

So when we're feeling like we are being overpowered by lies, we *can* walk in a place where we don't have to be overpowered by them. We don't let the lies mould and shape us; we turn from them towards the truth which sets us free. Romans 12:2 details part of our response to all that God has done for us, all the glorious gospel which the apostle Paul has set out in the first eleven chapters of Romans. Our response is to then present ourselves to God as an act of our worship and turn away from anything that the world would try to shape us with.

This is not just about turning away from outward behaviours such as no longer swearing or stealing, this is also about turning away from those thinking patterns that are based on lies. Those thinking patterns have moulded us to conform to the world's ways. As we turn away from the world's ways of thinking, the lies that come from our family history, the lies that have come from what we have been taught, maybe even in school, then God through the Spirit transforms us to be more and more the new creation we are meant to be. We are *metamorphosised,* we are free. Just as the caterpillar is gone and the butterfly emerges, so we are transformed into something new.

How many of us were taught that there is no God, that miracles don't happen today and that there is no life after death? One of my favourite songs of the moment is 'This I Believe' (The Creed) by Hillsong. It has lyrics that declare simple yet profound truths that daily I need to remind myself of. God is all-powerful, far beyond the power of any demonic influence or past experience, or even physical difficulty. I believe in Him and His power to set free, heal and restore. This is no lie, this is the real truth.

My biggest weakness was to think that I should not exist, I was nobody, no one, I was nothing, I was meant to be invisible and therefore I should blot myself out. That's a weakness, that's a button the enemy can push. But I don't need to be overpowered by that weakness anymore, because I can trust that God will give me the strength to overpower it. There comes a growing realisation that God is totally in control, He's totally the one we can trust, He's totally able to do the impossible and totally able to set us free. Now, that doesn't mean that I'm claiming healing as a 'right' or I'm claiming financial security and similar as a 'right' – I am not advocating the 'prosperity gospel' or the 'health, wealth' gospel. But God has given me everything I need to overpower the things that are trying to take me back into my weaknesses, trying to get me to look inwards again (2 Peter 1:3). That means that I have to trust that He is who He says He is.

We need to learn what our weaknesses are in order to be able to overcome the enemy, but it's also important for us to always remember our position in Christ. Often our weaknesses are the very things that God redeems and causes to be our strengths. In the book of Samuel we read how David said, 'I am weak today, though anointed king' (2 Samuel 3:39, NASB). He knew his weakness but he still knew he was king. It is important to come to the place of putting our hope, not in people, programmes or therapies and so on, but in God Himself. We have to learn to draw strength only from the Lord. Philippians 4:13 says, 'I can do all things through Him who strengthens me' (NASB). This strength comes not from people, pastors, close friends etc., but from God.

A real breakthrough in our lives comes when we learn to go first to a higher place for comfort, than to people. It's not that consulting people is wrong, we are of course part of a body, but ultimately we need to learn to be dependent upon God alone and run to Him rather than our first reaction being to cry on the shoulder of a friend.

Chapter Twenty-one: Having a Voice

Since those days of encountering deliverance, life has continued along with the journey of walking free. The mourning began to recede, the ashes began to be blown away and joy and praise began to take over. In the years since then, God has blessed us immensely, giving us a beautiful daughter and bringing amazing instantaneous healing to my spine, amongst many other things, but the biggest thing of all is that *Nemo* is dead. *Nemo* is no more and the mute now has a voice. The eternal life of our God has been at work to bring the life of the eternal to our everyday lives.

George Eldon Ladd wrote this:

> Has the realization gripped you that the very life of heaven itself dwells within you here and now? Did you ever know that? I am afraid that we live most of our life in terms of promise. We often sing of the future, and so we should sing. Our gospel is a gospel of glorious promise and hope. Yes, the best, the glorious best, is yet to be. And yet, we are not to live alone for the future. The future has already begun. The age to come has reached into this age; the kingdom of God has come unto you. The eternal life which belongs to tomorrow is here today. The fellowship which we shall know when we see Him face to face is already ours, in part but in reality. The transforming life of the Spirit of God which will one day transform our bodies has come to indwell us and to transform our characters and personalities.[5]

[5] George Eldon Ladd, *The Gospel of the Kingdom: Scriptural Studies in the Kingdom of God* (Grand Rapids, MI: Eerdmans, 1990).

All of us need to believe that God has the power to do whatever He wants to do. He can do the impossible. I feel as if I meet very few people today who *really* believe that God can totally change things, or bring about a miraculous healing, or give provision miraculously. There are so many ways in our Christian walk as churches where we give assent to God being a God of the impossible, but in practise we live as though we have to do it ourselves, or there's only 'so much' we can expect God for. Yet, if God can do it, He can do it! But we tend to have a boundary on what we are prepared to believe God can do, even though we agree that God can do the impossible. Yes, there's a difference between 'God can do it!' and 'Will He do it?' but that is about trust and knowing Him, knowing His voice. It is about relationship with God Himself – the Father.

We are to learn to recognise God's voice, He who speaks 'better things' (Hebrews 6:9), and line ourselves up with what He is saying. 'I can do all things through Him who strengthens me' (Philippians 4:13, NASB). So, for example, in the garden of Eden God clearly speaks. Adam and Eve hear His voice saying, 'you must not eat from the tree of the knowledge of good and evil' (Genesis 2:17). Then the enemy comes and whispers, 'Did God really say...?' (Genesis 3:1) and he begins to subtly twist what had been actually said. Eve at first reiterates what God had said but then listens to the enemy and believes him and eats. Then later Eve says, 'The snake deceived *me*' (Genesis 3:13, my emphasis) and shifts the blame. Eve acted on what she had listened to. This is how the enemy works with us. We can refute what the enemy says, and we can act on the basis of what God says, not on what the enemy whispers to us or what we tell ourselves from how we are feeling.

When Jesus was in the wilderness (Luke 4) He spoke back to the suggestions of the enemy with the truth. He sets us an example to follow, stating, 'It is written'.

When we feel bad, under attack or similar, we can take heart from how King David felt and hopefully deal with things as he did. Psalm 42:5-6 says:

> Why, my soul, are you downcast?
> Why so disturbed within me?
> Put your hope in God,
> for I will yet praise him,
> my Saviour and my God.
> My soul is downcast within me;
> therefore [or because of that] I will remember you [God] …

The Church is destined to be God's mouthpiece to the nations, and His hands and His feet, and the whole of His body. And it will happen, He will raise His Church up!

Currently, as I am writing this, we are all living through the Covid-19 worldwide pandemic. Every nation has been brought to a standstill in an effort to overcome devastating disease. The strange daily life of social distancing and isolation can bring up all our doubts and fears, all the issues we maybe would have been able to deal with in 'normal life'. For some it might be the first time issues to do with anxiety, depression, about 'how I fit in' and 'where I belong' have come to the fore. For me, it is yet another time for the enemy to try to resurrect *Nemo*, as memories of being locked in outbuildings and such are brought to my mind again, with similar emotions being evoked.

Our minds are amazing storehouses of information. Have you heard a song and instantly been transported mentally and emotionally to that special occasion when it was played for you? Or have you ever seen something such as a huge Alsatian dog and instantly felt fear as you are taken back to the day a dog like that bit you? This is what the mind does, it automatically responds to a situation you're in by reminding you of what went before. This is why some people struggle with post-traumatic stress; they hear or see something, or have a dream, and are instantly reliving the traumatic event which happened to them. This is what was happening for me, and I didn't realise until the power of that trauma was broken that I could speak back to the memory. So, in isolation, when the emotion associated with being locked away was revived by the power of my own mind, I could prevent the enemy getting on the back of this and pulling me back by my declaring, 'This is not pleasant but it is a new day. I am not being forcibly locked away as a punishment, I am being looked after for my own safety. The grace of God is abounding towards me and I am free to praise Him' – or something like that!

I can speak truth to myself and remind myself that 'the old has gone [and], the new is here' (2 Corinthians 5:17). The old taunts will come to us at different times in our lives but we can speak back to them.

Mother's ritual of telling me every day for one hour that I was mental and needed a doctor was carried out in front of an old fan heater when it was cold in the winter. During the years my sister and I had to care for her near the end of her life, we decided to take a little break together for a few days. During our break we went into an antiques shop and, as we were browsing in different parts of the store, I walked around a corner and suddenly a fan heater came into view. It was exactly the same as the one my mother had used. (Yes, I've reached the age when I see things from my own lifetime in antiques shops!)

I was instantly taken back to those days of hearing Mother's voice over and over telling me the same destructive stuff. I was reliving it all. But then my sister appeared and saw what I was looking at and heard me saying out loud, 'The old has gone, is finished, is dead, and the new has come.' She knew what was happening to me and added her voice to that by saying to me, 'That is all past now, it's gone.'

It is important that we learn not just to think the truth within ourselves, declaring truth to ourselves in our own thoughts, but that we speak it out. Where it is possible to speak out, I verbally assert, 'That is in the past now, that is gone.' Whatever we want to assert of the truth, it has more power when we verbalise it; we are reiterating it into our own mind, our own spirit, and the enemy hears that too. When I am alone, I can often be heard speaking seemingly into thin air, 'I am not listening to that, that is a lie, the truth is…' and then whatever I want to assert at that time. But it is not an empty exercise, I am speaking the truth, and my mind and my spirit will concur.

These instances which suddenly come to our recall are not the enemy at work, this is the power of our mind being prompted by what has been seen or heard. What we have to do when this happens is to then not allow the enemy to speak to us on the back of what the mind has been stimulated with, rather to remind ourselves that we are not bound by these things anymore. I then have to tell myself again that *Nemo* is dead, at the bottom of the baptism pool and I am new with a new identity in Christ.

Once again it is a time to speak the truth to ourselves, to declare to the enemy that 'I am a child of the King and brought into family, born into a chosen people for such a time as this'.[6] More than ever before, the world needs to hear the voice of the Church. There is no 'mute' button, no 'going back' option for the child of God, only the option to run the race for the prize that is ahead (1 Corinthians 9:24).

Recently I have felt my attention drawn to an incident in the life of the prophet Jeremiah. Having been shown by God that his people are going to be taken into captivity with the land falling into ruin, with no weddings not even any burials taking place and no fruitfulness left

[6] Queen Esther was given her position of influence 'for such a time as this' (see Esther 4:14).

in the land,[7] from his imprisonment, Jeremiah buys a field (Jeremiah 32). He then lives through that time but is always looking ahead to a time of restoration when God will bring fruitfulness back to the land. Instead of looking at all that was negative around him, instead of dwelling on his imprisonment, instead of seeing the futility in all that was happening in the world around him, instead of selling seemingly worthless pieces of land, Jeremiah does the opposite. He invests in the promise of fruitfulness and restoration to come by buying a field as a sign of what is to come, a new day of blessing.

Today we live in the midst of those end times of trouble and difficulty, but there are promises of hope for a new day that God has given for us to invest in. Romans 8:24-25 tells us that 'hope that is seen is no hope at all. Who hopes for what they already have? But if we hope for what we do not yet have, we wait for it patiently'. That is true hope.

Even in our lockdown, even in our seeming 'prison cells', even in life's difficulties, we are those who have a sure and certain hope (Hebrews 6:19). Even when the enemy would shout and lie to us of those things he has tried to shape in our lives, nevertheless we have been rescued. We are those who have been made alive, made new, set free, and now we have a voice. We will see the churches everywhere shining out like beacons of light and fire, filling the land and being a voice to the world. We are descended from Abraham's seed, a line of faith, and the promise that was to Abraham is now for us, that we will fill the whole earth and the nations will be blessed through us (Genesis 18:18; Genesis 22:18; Galatians 3:29). This was not just a promise for the nation of Israel but also for us who have been made heirs along with Israel (Ephesians 3:6).

God's kingdom will grow, filling the whole earth and toppling every other kingdom; we will see the earth filled with His glory (Habakkuk

[7] See Jeremiah 7:33-34; 16:7-9; 25:8-11.

2:14) and there will one day be those around the throne room from every tribe, and tongue and nation gathered to rejoice that a new day is come (Daniel 2:44; Revelation 7:9). We are those who now have a voice, and never has there been such a time as this to invest in His promises and let our voice be heard.

This is the message of this book – whatever you have gone through, however you feel, those things are neither your reality nor your hope; they no longer need to shape you. Your reality and your hope lie in the fact that now you are hidden in Christ Jesus, now you have been made new, now you are adopted into His family, and now you are a part of a chosen generation, a holy people (1 Peter 2:9), set apart for Him and, whoever you are, you now have a name and a voice to be heard and there is a new day coming to rejoice in.

This is the 'real' truth that will set you free and will give you a voice. Romans 5:17 in the NASB says:

> For if by the transgression of the one, death reigned through the one, much more those who receive the abundance of grace and of the gift of righteousness will reign in life through the One, Jesus Christ.

The Pearl

Secret wounds causing pain,
Busy days of stress and strain,
Drawing out the dross and dirt,
All of life a place of hurt.

Hidden away for none to see,
Deep within lies the key,
Flowing to the root of harm,
Comes an oil of healing balm.

Gone are all the hurts and smuts,
Filled and covered the deepest cuts.
Strong and bright this key comes forth,
Formed a pearl of greatest worth.

When every thing becomes a strain,
Remember what comes forth from pain.
A thing of beauty formed in thee,
A priceless pearl for all to see.

Ginny

HE WAS TEMPTED
LIKE AS WE ARE